M000083061

Single is the New Black

New Black

don't wear white 'til it's right

Dr. Karin Anderson Abrell

Copyright © 2015 Karin Anderson Abrell

Published by Clifton Hills Press, Valparaiso, Indiana

All rights reserved, including the right to reproduce this book or portions thereof in any form whatsoever. For information, please contact us at:

Clifton Hills Press
386 Deer Ridge Road
Valparaiso, Indiana 46385

Cover and interior art by Klocke Design

Author photo by Lauren Petersen

Printed in the United States of America

ISBN-13: 978-0915725-15-1
ISBN-10: 0-915725150

Praise for
Single is the New Black:

"Ditch the rules! Seriously. Enough of books trying to convince you that if you do this, say that, or act a certain way you'll hook the guy. How about just being yourself? Being single is not a curse or a crime or something that needs to be 'fixed', and *Single is the New Black* does a great job of reminding women that they are worthy of true love... whether solo or coupled."

— Kimberly Dawn Neumann, author of *The Real Reasons Men Commit: Why He Will – Or Won't – Love, Honor and Marry You*

"*Single is the New Black* blasts all ideas as to why you're still single. Instead of telling you exactly how to date (or how not to date), it encourages you to be yourself and keep on keeping on because if you're still single, it just hasn't happened for you. (At least not yet. But it totally will). Its words of encouragement are like talking amongst your friends. And it's all of the things we really need to hear when we're trying to navigate the single and dating world."

— Jess Downey, lifestyle blogger for
chaoticandcollected.com

Praise for the first edition of
Single is the New Black
(formerly titled *It Just Hasn't Happened Yet*)

"At last! A book that acknowledges that, while marriage can be a lovely thing, it need not be the holy grail for single women. Reading *It Just Hasn't Happened Yet* is like spending time with a wise, funny, loving girlfriend who genuinely has your best interest at heart."

> — Cary Barbor, writer for *Match.com* and former health editor, *More* Magazine

"Funny, breezy, and oh-so-practical—a sorely-needed sanity check in a relationship-crazed world."

> — Leslie Talbot, author of *Singular Existence: Because It's Better to Be Alone Than to Wish You Were!*

"It's a clearly thought out book, with a lot of great advice on how we may not have found the one yet, but that's not a reason to settle for whoever comes along next... Karin's insight into the world of why people ask us these at times rude and embarrassing questions is truly worth a read. She's light-hearted and funny, yet full of worthwhile information."

— Amanda Perkins, Urban Bachelorette
at *www.urbanbachelorette.com*

"What sets apart Karin Anderson's new book... is a glorious lack of blame, accompanied by a daring refusal to fix anyone's problems... Anderson... strenuously resists the idea that single women are by definition doing 'something wrong,' and in fact advocates a healthy acceptance of whatever relationship status a woman happens to find herself in."

— Paula Carino at *www.breakupgirl.net*

"It Just Hasn't Happened Yet is a Must Read. Written as a conversation between girlfriends, mothers and daughters, young (and not so young) women and a guy friend or some experts, the book demolishes all the advice in most self-help books for singles, while illustrating all the negative social pressures on single women. Dr. Anderson's perspective challenges single women, and all those around them, to change their viewpoint. It's fun and informative."

— Dr. E. Kay Trimberger, sociologist
and author, *The New Single Woman*

For Dan
You were more than worth the wait.

Table of Contents

Part 1

ridiculous comments you hear and how to deal with them

Preface

A few years ago I was 40 years old and single without a man in sight.

Everyone had an opinion as to why I wasn't married. I was too picky, too intimidating, too focused on my career, too neurotic, too analytical, and too sensitive. There had to be something wrong with me, right? Otherwise, I'd be married like everyone else my age.

But despite the accusations, I felt pretty darn normal.

Still, I wanted to be proactive so I headed to the self-help section for advice and encouragement.

Wrong move.

Titles in the dating/relationship genre provided more shame than support and more disparagement than empowerment. They firmly reinforced the "something's wrong with you" message, insisting I needed to resolve all my relationship issues and unearth any man-repelling pathologies if I ever hoped to find love.

I didn't buy it—the message (or the books.)

Where was the voice of reason? Couldn't anyone else see the obvious—that we can't control every aspect of our lives and in many cases people are single simply because they have yet to meet the right person? Why couldn't relationship experts just acknowledge this reality? And where was the book applauding singles for refusing to settle and having the strength to go it alone?

Well, I couldn't find that book. So I wrote it.

And then, all of a sudden, it happened for me— I met the love of my life. I never could have envisioned finding a man so perfect for me. I put it this way in a song I wrote for him, "You're more than I had ever dared to dream."

And here's the kicker, I didn't have to change a thing about myself. He fell in love with me *exactly* the way I am.

Sappy, right? So why am I telling you all this?

Reason #1:

It's *absolutely*, *positively* worth waiting for the right one!

Reason #2:

People pick up a self-help book looking for solutions. Therefore my thesis—that you're fine "as is"—is, admittedly, rather unconventional for the dating/relationship genre.

But now that I've met my husband I'm able to say with certainty that I was right all along. I stayed true to myself and didn't change. I thrived as a single adult, loved my life and worked on becoming the best Karin possible, and eventually, at the age of 40, I met a man who's the perfect one for me.

Disclaimers

In preparing for this book I've received two questions I'd like to address here.

Q: "Dr. Karin, you're a psychologist for Pete's sake. Why would you encourage dysfunctional single women to stay screwed up? They'll never snag a man if they're full on cray cray! Why don't you give them some good advice so they can at least *try* to be normal?"

A: The theme of this book in no way suggests that single women are perfect with no need to work on themselves. Of course they have issues! They're human! Single women should strive to become the very best possible versions of themselves. But so should married couples, divorcées, and those who never wish to marry.

The point is, your friends didn't have to become perfect before Mr. Right showed up. They found a man (who was also flawed, by the way) who liked their unique blend of "great and crazy".

Besides, even if you did somehow miraculously become perfect, that's still no guarantee Mr. Wonderful would immediately walk through the door. But that's what other books essentially promise—"stop being such a nut job and your knight will ride up on his white horse tomorrow." It's a load of bunk and we all know it, but it sells books. So, I'm providing an alternate vantage point.

Q: "You seem to think all single people are dying to get married. Newsflash—some of us prefer living solo. Marriage isn't for everyone, you know. Plus, your position contributes to the prevailing pejorative stereotypes depicting single people as miserable, lonely, and desperate. Why would you want to perpetuate such stigma?"

A: To those single folks who love living *la vida solo* and have no interest in ever finding a spouse: I applaud you. I admire you. I champion your choice. And since you're perfectly happy, feel free to give this book to a friend because it's not for you. I wrote it for singles in pursuit of a partner—for women who tire of hearing what's wrong with them and are weary of the accusations. It's for those who want to get married and sometimes worry it will never happen.

Author's Note

Though all the scenes in this book actually occurred, the names, ages, and other identifying information regarding the individuals involved have been changed.

Introduction

Single is the new black. No, really—it is. Currently, the majority of American adults (50.2%) are unmarried.[1] So, statistically speaking, single is the "new normal". But it sure doesn't feel that way. Despite changing demographics, singles remain stigmatized and marginalized.

Social psychologist, Dr. Bella DePaulo, coined the term *singlism* to describe this discrimination. "If you are single, you lose by definition. No matter what you can point to on your own behalf—spectacular accomplishments, a lifelong and caring convoy of relatives and friends, extraordinary altruism—none of it redeems you if you have no soulmate. Others will forever be scratching their heads and wondering what's wrong with you and comparing notes (he's always been a bit strange; she's so neurotic; I think he's gay)."[2]

So finally, here's a book to help you deal with such nonsense!

In Part 1, we'll dismantle the ridiculousness you put up with—from accusations that it's your fault you're single to clichés contending you'd immediately meet The One if you'd just get back "out there".

In Part II, we'll examine ways we sometimes make things harder on ourselves, such as a tendency to get stuck in on-again/off-again relationships, and the reckless choices made from the fear of being alone.

Part III provides a few words of wisdom from those who've been there—from women who braved years in the dating scene and experienced the sting of *singlism,* but stayed true to themselves.

Key

Every chapter consists of the same format, so here's a key to help you follow along:

PSYCH 101

In this section, I analyze the chapter's theme so we can observe it more clearly and better understand our feelings and responses. I call it Psych 101, but it's not a boring college lecture—promise!

It just hasn't happened yet

After objectively examining the situation, I get back to the parts that are nevertheless annoying and help figure out ways to deal with them.

Ditto

Here's where someone else speaks to the issue at hand. She may be a writer, researcher, or a fellow single woman putting up with the same stuff. It sure helps to know you're not alone.

Girl Talk

In this section, I receive a letter related to the chapter's topic. Sometimes the writer agrees with me, sometimes she doesn't, but we hash it out, woman-to-woman.

The Awful Truth

The scripts presented in this segment depict (unfortunately) a "slice of life". Each one describes an actual scenario encountered by a single woman. And, as the title suggests, it ain't pretty.

Guy Talk

Well, I figured we should get the male perspective, right? This book talks a lot about guys, so it seemed prudent to let one have the floor from time to time.

Selfie

A brief snapshot of my personal life as it relates to the chapter's topic.

Shout Out!

My final words of encouragement to you.

Part 1

ridiculous comments you hear and
how to deal with them

chapter 1

It's Not Your Fault!

so stop beating yourself up!

I'm totally fed up hearing comments implying there's something wrong with me just because I don't have a man—statements like that are hurtful! It's really sad that people see being single as meaning there's something wrong with you, and I'm so over all the lame advice about how to meet someone!

— Allison, 26

It's not your fault you're still single. Yes, you read that correctly. Read it again if you need to. Let it sink in. You haven't done *anything* wrong and you don't need to change *anything* about yourself in order to find The One. Seriously. I know some of you don't believe me and it may take the entire book for you to internalize this, but it's not your fault you haven't met him. It just hasn't happened yet.

Not that I'm surprised by your resistance. I know what I'm up against. You probably aren't hearing this sort of perspective anywhere else. In fact, if you've been single for any length of time, you've likely endured plenty of allegations bearing the exact

14

opposite sentiment. Friends ask about your relationships in a sleuth-like manner, searching for clues as to where you're screwing up: "So, what exactly happened with Kevin? I thought this one was finally working out..." Sometimes their teasing subtly veils accusations: "Honey, what's going on? You always chase the good ones away!" or "Have you ever thought about getting a little therapy to figure this stuff out?" Then again, the occasional aunt, brother, or coworker blatantly accuses, "You're way too _____! No wonder you're still single!"

Even if you're lucky enough to have sensitive friends and strong family support, you still get hit by the antagonistic portrayals of single women so firmly embedded in our mass media and pop culture. Consider chick flicks depicting quirky, lovelorn women who, after Pygmalion-esque metamorphoses, emerge "fixed" and finally suitable for marriage. Or flip through the latest issue of any number of women's magazines. Notice the attention devoted to helping single women identify "Dating Don'ts" and relationship *faux pas*—articles such as "Stop Scaring Him Off: The Real Reason He Didn't Call" or "Needy Moves You Must Nix: Nine Ways Women Come Off as Too Dependent".

By our late twenties, if not sooner, we get the picture—something's drastically wrong with us or else we'd have already snagged ourselves a man. Caving under the onslaught of messages from rom coms, fashion mags, and our Aunt Barbara, we internalize the undesirable truth. "Face it," we tell ourselves, "the common denominator in all my failed relationships is *me*. I'm doing something wrong. It's my fault I'm single."

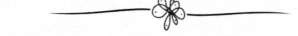

PSYCH 101: WHY WE DO IT

Why do we blame ourselves? Why take the brunt of it? Why believe it's entirely our fault we're still single?

Actually, there's a bit of twisted logic at work here. By blaming ourselves, we gain a measure of control. That's right. Rather than revealing some inveterate self-loathing, the masochistic "blame game" merely exposes a need for control. *Thanks*, you're saying. *Now you're calling us all control freaks*.

Well, maybe not freaks, but we do like our control. It's only natural. Think about it. In today's world, women have more command over more areas of our lives than ever before. We take charge of our education, strategically maneuver our career, and independently manage our finances. When things go wrong in one of these areas, we know who the culprit is—us! We've dropped the ball or taken a wrong turn. So when something's amok in our love life (such as, we don't have one), we come to the same conclusion: we must have screwed it up.

In targeting ourselves, we begin a nasty regimen of self-blame that, although a bit painful at first, ultimately produces hope. *Wait,* you're saying, *blame leads to hope? Exactly how does that work?* Simple. It puts the control in our hands, right where we like it. We tell ourselves, *If I'm the one ruining my love life, then I'm the one who can fix it. All I have to do is go to Barnes & Noble, find the right book, and become an entirely different person! Then I'll find true love and lasting happiness. Problem solved!*

I mean, consider the alternative. If it's not our fault we're single, who gets the blame? God? Fate? The Universe? These forces lie well beyond our jurisdiction. If they're responsible, there's nothing we can do about it. But if it's our misstep, we can correct it.

So, while I hate hearing my smart, sexy, savvy, single friends berate themselves for tragic flaws, tacky habits, and troublesome neuroses, I get it. I get why they adopt this diffident demeanor and denounce their defects. The self-inflicted sucker punches are well worth it; they allow us to feel in control.

It just hasn't happened yet

But just because I get it doesn't mean I support it. It's tough enough that our love lives haven't played out as planned, yet we go and exacerbate the situation by accusing ourselves of ruining our chances for romance. More pain!

And to control the situation we try to correct the "problem" by taking charge as we would at the office. We conduct a needs-based assessment, identify weaknesses, and submit a detailed analysis with suggestions for revision—all in anticipation of increased outcomes.

Except in this case, the *needs-based assessment* is conducted on us. The *weaknesses identified* target our core, unique qualities. *Suggestions for revision* may or may not be realistic. *Increased outcomes?* After ripping our egos to shreds, I don't think so.

How cruel! Guilty of destroying our love lives we scrutinize ourselves, pin-pointing some random personality trait, physical imperfection, or emotional idiosyncrasy that *must* go in order for us to prove acceptable to the opposite sex? Talk about kicking a girl when she's down!

And the worst part? We're not controlling a darn thing. We're just beating ourselves up. This exercise in masochism doesn't bring us any closer to love and happiness. Give me a break! All we've done is lowered our self-esteem in efforts to correct a situation that, actually, we can't do anything about anyway. Nice.

Ditto

Take heart, it's nothing personal. Even the most beautiful, sophisticated, and talented single women are suspect, women like *über* successful Sheryl Crow who recounts this exchange when she ran into another well-known personality and heard, "I was just thinking about you the other day! I was thinking she's such a great girl, why doesn't she get married and have kids?"

Crow's reaction? "I felt like the breath rushed out of my body. I couldn't believe somebody was actually voicing what most of America probably thinks of me. I know it seems odd to people—if you're not married by a certain age you're either gay, asexual, or a freak who can't get along with anybody."[3]

Writer Suzanne Schlosberg puts it this way, "In your thirties you dread taking your place at the Singles Table. Your singleness has started to feel like something more serious than the flu, something chronic, painful and obscure—like diverticulitis. Deep down you know you haven't done anything to cause your condition, but you know that other people suspect it's your fault and in your worst moments you start to wonder if they're right."[4]

Girl Talk

Dear Karin,

So, you're saying it's not my fault I'm single and I love that—I'm totally down with the message. All this girl power stuff is really cute and all, but in my case, I am the problem. It is my fault I'm single.

To be honest, I'm kind of a freak when it comes to relationships. I always end up destroying them. Obviously I don't mean to; it's just that when I'm dating someone and getting to know him, I want to be around him all the time. I get totally caught up in it. But it always backfires because my boyfriends tell me I'm clingy and insecure—which I am! Of course this usually pushes them away. Guys hate the whole "needy" thing. So I end up getting dumped. See, I told you, it is my fault! I can admit it, but I can't seem to change it!

Like I said, I love the book's concept, the whole "I'm OK, you're OK" thing, very empowering for women, but it doesn't apply to me. I'm not OK. Really, I'm not!

— Daisy, 31

Dear Daisy,

Obviously the "I'm not OK" stance is workin' for you, and I'd be loath to rip away that comfy security blanket of yours, but I've got to take issue with one point. You've decided you're too needy and clingy and that this horrible trait pushes guys away. Your Saran Wrap approach to relationships does you in every time, is that it?

Well, I bet you're right. I'm sure you're as needy as the day is long—a complete leech! I can see it now—a guy merely glances your way and you latch on like white on rice. And if your new "boyfriend" (as in some guy you talked to for five minutes at the bar last Saturday) doesn't call or text you ten times a day, you flip.

So sure, I bet you do push *some* guys away. But those guys—well, they're the *wrong* guys, at least for you. See, I guarantee there are women right now in happy, loving relationships who are *way* more needy than you could ever be. They just happened to find their match and someday you will, too. It's really that simple.

So, cling away! In doing so, you'll naturally weed out the fellas who want a more independent woman and eventually, a guy looking for a needy, clingy, suck-the-life-outta-ya chick is gonna sop you up with a biscuit!

— Karin

The Awful Truth

The title of this section says it all. These scenes are not *based* on real stories. They *are* real stories!

WOMEN'S INHUMANITY TO WOMEN

CAST.

REBECCA: 37-year-old marketing director. Single.

ELLEN: 42-year-old freelance writer. Married with one child.

DEBBIE: 35-year-old stay-at-home mom with three children. On hiatus from a job in sales.

INTERIOR — HOTEL BANQUET HALL — DAY

Rebecca, Ellen, and Debbie are attending a luncheon at the national convention of the Organization for Women Leaders and Entrepreneurs.

> ELLEN
> Hey, does anyone know if Audrey Landry was able to make it to convention?

REBECCA

No, I don't think she could come this year.

DEBBIE

That's too bad. I was hoping to catch up with her and make sure she's doing okay.

REBECCA

Okay? Last I heard she was doing great! She'd just earned a big promotion at work and was headed to grad school in the fall.

DEBBIE

Well, that's good to know, but I was thinking more about her personal life. Things haven't been going well. She never seems to have a boyfriend and it doesn't make sense. She's so intelligent and beautiful and fun to be with!

ELLEN

Yeah, what's going on with her? She's got to be 26 or 27 by now. You'd think a girl like her would have been snatched up long ago!

DEBBIE

I can't figure it out either. It's crazy that an amazing woman like Audrey isn't married already! Too bizarre! What's the problem?

REBECCA

Um, actually she's been dating a guy for over a year now and they just moved in together.

ELLEN and DEBBIE let out a collective, audible sigh of relief.

DEBBIE

Thank goodness! I really was beginning to wonder what was wrong.

Lesson Learned: Even among members of a women's leadership organization—which by definition is dedicated to the development of women per their career aspirations and entrepreneurial goals—the most important information about you is your relationship status. And your associates will be so concerned (read: obsessed) about it, they may gossip about you when you're not there and worse yet, in the presence of another member who happens to be older than you and further "off" the relational mark.

Guy Talk

Okay. Karin's totally right about the whole "you're fine just the way you are" thing and I've got the perfect example for you.

I used to know this girl, Abby, right? And let's just say she had a little junk in the trunk—and the back seat, and the passenger's side, and the— (Okay, okay, we get it! — Karin) Anyway, she was always complaining about how guys only want thin women and she'd go on and on about how men never asked her out and how they found her unattractive and immediately relegated her to the friend category. She was always like, "Guys are so shallow! They only like skinny chicks! I can't be anorexic, I already tried! Blah, blah, blah..."

Well, one day, this guy, Rick, starts working at my job. He's like a total partier and he has this cookout at his place a couple weeks after he got hired. So my buddies and I go over to throw a couple sausages on the grill or whatever. After a minute, I went inside to find his john—which was hard to do because I had to climb over all his crap 'cause this guy was a complete slob. Anyway, I literally stumbled upon a box of old pictures and there's this hilarious shot of Rick all awkward in a tux and this girl in a prom dress with big hair and, let's just say, plenty of other big features, if you know what I mean...

This little pictorial retrospective clued me in to his "preferences" when it comes to the ladies. I called Abby and invited her to meet up with us. The rest is history.

— **Guy**

Um, okay then. Well, personally I wouldn't have used that example but I've got to admit this story substantiates my point and, true, I did solicit a guy's perspective...

— Karin

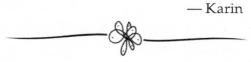

Selfie

For the majority of my single life, I blamed myself.

It started in high school, where I dismissed boys my age (stuck-up girl!) while mooning over my older brother's friends (silly girl!). Then in college I crushed the heart of the best boyfriend I'd ever had (stupid girl!), who eventually got fed up with our on-again/off-again relationship and left me in our mid-twenties for a woman who could commit. Consequently, I beat myself up for years—I'd been a stuck-up, silly, stupid girl and that's why I was still single.

As thirty loomed, I became increasingly despondent, convinced I'd ruined my only chance for love. I'd berate myself with self-talk—*How many really exceptional guys do you think are out there, Karin? You trashed a once-in-a-lifetime relationship and have no one to blame but yourself. You'll never be in love like that again.* I resigned myself to believing that some people find true love while others don't. Apparently, I fell into the latter category.

And it was all my fault.

Shout Out!

So to my smart, sexy, savvy singletons I say this: You aren't screwed up, it's not your fault, and no matter how much you pointlessly admonish yourselves, the whole deal is out of your control anyway. You can't hurry love—it just hasn't happened yet. And that's perfectly fine... because single is the new black!

chapter 2

Your Mother Is Wrong!

*you don't need to lose 10 pounds or
wear a little more make-up*

*My mom always tells me that the good ones are
getting snatched up left and right and I better
get my act together before they're all gone.
Doesn't she understand? I'd love to meet a nice
guy and get married. All the pressure she puts
on me doesn't help. It just makes me feel like
I'm disappointing her and letting her down.*

— Kendra, 30

Mothers. They mean well, of course, but wow,
can they work our nerves! Even the most innocent
interactions between a single daughter and her mom
feel loaded with ulterior motives and hidden messages.
Are we hypersensitive in assuming her every utterance
contains oblique instructions as to how we might more
readily procure a husband? Do our single daughter
antennae detect criticism in seemingly benign advice
and censure in innocent suggestions? Are we paranoid
or is this our reality?

Certainly, I can't speak for the entire demographic, but a solid majority of mothers of single women spend a decent amount of time bemoaning their daughter's marital status. Since they ruminate over our spinsterhood so much, they come up with countless explanations as to what we're doing to keep the gentlemen away. We're too independent or too dependent, too intimidating or too withdrawn, too aggressive or too passive, too opinionated or too shy. Too *something*.

Note also how the rules have changed since your younger days. When you were in high school, your mom called you "fast" for wearing too much black eye liner. Now she swears you'd meet a nice boy if you just put a little color on your cheeks. Back then, she encouraged you to choose your boyfriends carefully, since none of the hoodlums you brought home were good enough for you anyway. Now, she claims you're too picky and pressures you to pursue every fool who glances your way. Then, she made you change your clothes if you tried to wear something too daring. Now, she insists you don't "doll up" enough.

And of course, there's always, "Whatever happened to that nice young man, Howie Johnston? He comes from such a good family and has a very bright future at the law firm. I know he was sweet on you. Why didn't you ever give him a chance?

Honestly! If you think you're too good for everyone, you'll end up alone!"

We can't win, you know. Even if we have a boyfriend, we're still doing something wrong. We're with the wrong guy (again) so she commences with "Lecture Series A: Why You Keep Picking Liars and Losers". Or we're with the right guy (finally) and she proceeds to "Lecture Series B: Selecting the Perfect Ultimatum to Make Your Boyfriend Propose". Naturally, both speeches are peppered with reminders about our ticking biological clock, warning that we're completely fooling ourselves if we think *in vitro* fertilization will solve everything, and besides, if we really loved her, we'd show a little concern for her lifelong desire for grandchildren. Somehow your brother's four kids don't count.

PSYCH 101: WHY SHE DOES IT

Remember, your mother operates with the mindset of another generation and another era. Sure, she made it to the new millennium, but her worldview harkens back a cool thirty or forty years. In my case, my mother represents the classic woman of the fifties—devoted wife and mother. She even majored in home economics in college—and yes, it was a real major at the time. She began her senior year in the fall of 1957, terrified of reaching for a diploma at commencement with a ring-less left hand. Though just 21, she dreaded the thought of moving alone to a new town and embarking upon her teaching career as a single woman. People would pity her! And besides, how would she ever find a nice boy once she left college? Thankfully, just in the nick of time, she met my father and pulled off a "co-ed coup"—graduated in May and married in June.

Part of your mom's energy about your singleness could be a projection of how *she* would have felt if she were in your shoes. Many of our mothers couldn't have survived the single life. They just wouldn't have done it. They would have married anyone to avoid the stigma of being an "old maid"—a lovely moniker they'd have earned at the tender age of 23, by the way. I don't judge our mothers; theirs was a different era, after all. The pressure to marry and have children must have been overwhelming in the 1950s, 1960s, and 1970s. We still feel it today. Imagine what it was like then!

Your mom may also see your single status as a reflection on her parenting. Somehow, she must have failed you. At times, she questions herself—"How did I end up raising a spinster daughter? Where did I go wrong? Did I neglect to teach her the art of flirting? I knew I shouldn't have let her play soccer on the boys' team in second grade!" Parents begin to second-guess their child-rearing practices when things don't turn out as planned. Part of the reason she keeps rushing you to get married might be an attempt to let herself off the hook. Once you wed, she can breathe a sigh of relief and feel assured she did a good job raising you.

Then again, if your mom hails from the baby-boom generation, she may pressure you for different reasons. She was no Donna Reed after all! Exactly the opposite, as a matter of fact. While you were growing up, she indoctrinated you in all things ERA, boasting of rallies, marches, and burned bras. Bedtime stories included excerpts from the writings of Gloria Steinem and Betty Friedan. Your mom declared you could do it all, have it all, and be anything you wanted *sans* a man. Please—by age 5, you knew you needed a man like a fish needs a bicycle.

But now, as you enter your 30s, she's starting to renege. Like the 1950s-era mother, she begins to doubt herself. "Maybe it's my fault she's still single. Did I have to force-feed her all that feminism? I'm sure I overdid it. I could have let her keep at least one of her Barbie's bikinis. And insisting that her Ken doll wear a 'Men are Pigs' t-shirt at all times was probably a little much." Looking back, she wonders if she did you a disservice. All that feminist rhetoric, while fun to toss around at book clubs and cocktail parties, won't keep you warm at night.

In addition, regardless of your mother's generation, she's probably experiencing a bit of peer pressure. That's right. Unfortunately, it survives long after high school. Very likely, your mom takes a hit or two about your singleness from various "friends" who see your maiden status as evidence that something is drastically wrong in your mom's perfect little family. These so-called friends may even enjoy seeing her obvious angst when discussing your husband-less existence. Heck, some probably look for opportunities to make her squirm. These women are the type who bump into your mom at the grocery store and immediately go for the jugular—*your* love life. "How's Jenny? Is she seeing anyone special?" Subtext: "Sure, things look good from the outside, but your daughter can't hang onto a man! Something must be wrong with her. Clearly, you're not such a great mother after all!" Of course, such women never ask your mom about your career, hobbies, travels, or volunteer work. They care about one thing: marriage. And until you're married, your mom has failed. Sadly, women can be catty at any age.

So when your mom puts the pressure on, remember, there may be more behind it than you realize.

It just hasn't happened yet

Your mom's the control freak this time. And plenty of unfortunate fallout results from this way of thinking. First off, it's sad your mom feels bad and that she imagines she's to blame for your singleness. That's quite a burden for her to carry around. Secondly, it's regrettable that her efforts to correct her misdoings involve offering you various suggestions as to how you could change yourself to find Mr. Right. Great tactic, because it leads to the third part of this sad situation. Now you feel bad because your mom criticizes you and implies something's wrong with you. Though she means well, the message remains, "You're flawed. Figure out how to fix it so you can find a man."

Ditto

Don't worry, help is on the way! Researchers in sociology and psychology are beginning to tackle the subject of single adulthood—even down to the part about single women and their nagging mothers! In her book *The New Single Woman*, sociologist and author E. Kay Trimberger states,

"Mothers of single women over the age of thirty-five often impose the coupled ideal on their daughters. Today it is commonplace for a mother to brag about the educational accomplishments of her twenty-seven-year-old single daughter. But the mother of a fifty-year-old ever-single daughter often has very different feelings. She frequently says, 'I worry about Janet's being alone. I wish she would meet someone and settle down.' How often do we hear a mother say, 'I'm so proud of Janet; she bought her own home, won a teaching award last year, and has more friends than anyone I know'?"[5]

Girl Talk

Dear Karin,

Let me just lay this out for you. This chapter may make sense for Gentiles, but clearly you don't understand the Jewish mother—they're way more intense! Not only is it her <u>right</u> to find you the man of <u>her</u> dreams, but it's basically her entire reason for being! Oy! There's absolutely no getting through to her. Maybe some moms' behavior can be explained by this business about generational differences and middle-aged peer pressure, but a Jewish mother unloads every ounce of guilt she's feeling onto her daughter. And if her matchmaking schemes don't work out, she takes it as a personal affront. She's just plain ruthless!

From my mom's perspective, I'm continually ruining my love life. She swears I'm too aggressive and that I need to let men take the lead. But then the next thing I know, she's forcing me on some guy she wants me to meet and complaining I'm being too timid and not pursuing him hard enough.

35

Then she nags me about my weight every time I see her, but gets all hurt if I don't help myself to seconds and thirds of her brisket when I come over for dinner. And she never asks me about my job or my friends; all she can talk about is getting me married to a nice Jewish boy—SOON!

Oh, and by the way, his name is Howie Silverman, not Johnston, and my mother has never met him, but he's the nephew of my parents' accountant and she's heard he's very handsome and very smart.

— Sarah, 34

Dear Sarah,

Shiksa that I am, I may have missed a few cultural nuances to the mom issue, but I've got to believe there's hope for *all* moms and daughters. Maybe your mom needs to read this chapter. A few times. And then a few more. Perhaps she should commit it to memory?

— Karin

The Awful Truth

Remember, these scenes are not *based* on real stories. They *are* real stories!

SHELF LIFE

CAST.
LISA: single 35-year-old restaurant manager
JOSEPHINE: her mother

INTERIOR — ITALIAN RESTAURANT — NIGHT

> JOSEPHINE
> As another year comes to a close,
> I want to make a toast to my
> hopes and aspirations for my
> family... For my daughter, Lisa, a
> toast to her finding the husband of
> her dreams who will bring her all
> the happiness she deserves.

> LISA
> Oh, Mom, come on. You know I'm
> perfectly happy.

> JOSEPHINE
> Maybe so, but you still need a
> husband.

> LISA
> Yeah, well, I had one of those and
> we saw how that worked out.

JOSEPHINE
Lisa, you act as if you don't ever
want to be married again!

LISA
Well, Mom, I'm not really sure
that I do.

Josephine freezes dramatically. She's unsure
as to what to make of this.

JOSEPHINE
May I be frank here?

LISA
And when have you ever *not* been
frank, Mom?

JOSEPHINE
Honey, you really don't know what
you're talking about. Sure, it's all
fun and games now because you
can live it up and date a different
man every night. But you have to
realize this won't last forever.
Think about it! You're only 35, so
you're still quite attractive, but
how long do you really think your
looks will hold up?

Lesson learned: Single women have a shelf life. According to Lisa's mom, after about 35, our physical appearance deteriorates dramatically. So even if we're completely happy and content, we better get serious about locking in a husband because at some point in the future we may want one, but our looks will have expired and it'll be way too late.

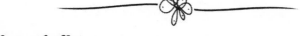

Guy Talk

Listen. I'm obviously not a mother or a daughter and never will be. I think I'll pass the ball to my mom on this one. I've got a sister who just turned 30 and my mom's been pretty irritated with Karin recently for, as she puts it, brainwashing her.

— Guy

Mom Talk

Good, because I've got plenty to say on the subject. Honestly, Karin, I'd appreciate it if you stopped filling my daughter's head with all this nonsense—telling her she's fine just the way she is! If she were fine, she'd be married like all my friends' 30-year-old daughters. Please, what do you know? You didn't get married until 42!

Now you listen to me! I love my daughter and I know what's best for her. And what's best for her is that she finds herself a nice husband to settle down with and start a family. And that's what she wants, too. You act like she's happy being single! She's not! She's very lonely!

And you could have been a little gentler with your treatment of mothers. Then again, you're not a mom so you can't possibly understand what it's like for us to watch our daughters go through heartbreak after heartbreak and get hurt time and time again. It's very painful for us! If we get a little pushy about finding the right guy, it's only because we worry so much. We're not getting any younger either, you know. Is it so wrong to want our daughters married and settled down before we die?

You think you're helping her with all this foolishness about her being fine the way she is, but that's not going to get her down the aisle any faster. In fact, it will probably slow things down. She <u>needs</u> to feel a sense of urgency. It'll help her focus on getting her priorities straight and meeting her future husband!

— Guy's Mom

Guy's Mom,

Sorry, but I can't align with you on this one. You're saying you want your daughter happy, but I'm telling you, you're totally stressing her out with all the pressure you're putting on her! And as I mentioned in the chapter, you're also making her feel cruddy. Is that *really* what you want to do to her?

I know you think if she just got serious about finding a husband, she would. And you've probably nagged her to sign up for an online dating site or check out the church ice-cream social or maybe you've dropped a subtle hint at Christmas with a stocking full of "How to Nab a Man" self-help books.

I've got one word for you: STOP. Just stop it. Enjoy your daughter. Love her. Be grateful for her. Embrace every aspect of her—not just her marital status. She's fine just the way she is and one of these days, she'll meet him. It's just a matter of time.

That's right. She'll meet "The One" and rush home to introduce you to your future son-in-law. At first, you'll adore him. After all, he's the knight in shining armor come to rescue your princess from spinsterhood! Eventually, though, the newness will wear off and you'll wistfully think back to those precious days when you had your daughter all to yourself. Why? Because once you have a SON-IN-LAW, you become a MOTHER-IN-LAW. And we all know what that's about!

— Karin

P.S. As for the getting her settled down before you die thing? Look at it this way. If you truly can't depart this earth without seeing your daughter hitched, then apparently she's doing her part to keep you alive and kickin'!

Selfie

Ultimately, my mom was pretty great throughout my single years.

As I mentioned earlier, my mom epitomizes the classic 1950s woman, so it's rather impressive that she was able to encourage my career aspirations and refrain from nagging too much about my love life.

However, she did get plenty of flak from her friends regarding my single status. Over the years, she repeatedly heard comments along the lines of, "Karin must be way too picky" and "I don't understand what the boys aren't seeing in your daughter!"

Occasionally, I'd hear the jabs first hand. One year when I went home for Christmas, my mom's friend, Sandy, couldn't wait to tell us about her daughter's engagement. My mother and I expressed our enthusiasm for the good news. But Sandy couldn't resist throwing a zinger my way.

"I thought you might have a ring by now, too, Karin."

I explained that my boyfriend and I had only been dating a year.

"Well, Justine and Bob have only been together seven months," Sandy replied.

I had no idea how to respond to that. Three or four very impolite retorts came to mind but I stuffed the snarky comebacks, mumbled something about taking my time, and changed the subject.

Interestingly, these same women often asked my mom to set me up with their sons. But if I didn't instantly hit it off with their precious baby boy, my mom would endure the brunt of it, sometimes putting a strain on her friendships. Eventually I asked her to decline any more overtures toward "mother matchmaking". I didn't want my love life negatively affecting my mother's relationships.

Shout Out!

So to my smart, sexy, savvy, singletons I say this: Stay strong no matter how much your mom nags you. This may be the first time ever, but in this case, your mother is wrong! Naturally, she's eager to shop for wedding gowns, but does she *really* want you in white before it's right? Of course not! Next time she starts in on the subject tell her not to worry... because single is the new black!

chapter 3

You're Not Too Picky!

you're choosing a life partner—
aren't you supposed to be selective?

A single woman should accept herself for who she is and never bend down to anybody's standards. Follow your heart, and do what you know is right for yourself. And yeah, I've been called picky. But what should I do, just grab any Tom, Dick, or Harry off the street?

— Kimberly, 29

This one's a gem. *You're too picky.* Every woman I know who's been single for any period of time has heard it. If you haven't gotten it yet, you will. Just wait.

Be aware, it may come at you in another form. *You're too picky* can disguise itself in a comment like *You don't give guys a chance!* Or *You're awfully critical of the men you date!* Or *You really need to be more realistic!*

Realistic about what? What exactly are people trying to tell us? How are we supposed to take comments like this? Obviously, I was on the receiving end of such statements, too, so I don't really know, but let's explore some plausible subtexts. "You're too picky" might mean:

- Apparently, you *think* you're pretty special, but you're no better than anyone else. It's time you considered lowering your standards.

- You're no spring chicken! At this point, you need to be grateful for whoever you can get!

- Sure, I got to marry the love of my life. But that's not gonna happen for you. Sorry 'bout your luck!

- You must not see yourself clearly. You're aiming way out of your league. These homely sorts we set you up with are more your pace.

And these are our *friends* who say such things to us?

Let me get this straight. When you're 23, you're allowed to be picky. In fact, you're encouraged to select suitors carefully. Everyone tells you how smart, beautiful, and exceptional you are. You're a catch! You *should* be discriminating! But, as the years go on and you enter your 30s, people begin to chastise your choice to remain choosy. In fact, you've become a bit bothersome with your whole "I just want to wait for the right one" attitude. It's time to meet a guy, get married, and be done with it already!

How offensive and insulting to suggest that, because you're older than 25 or 35 or 45 or whatever arbitrary number someone designates as a cut off, you need to be satisfied with whatever schmo comes your way! *Oops! I just celebrated my 36th birthday and everyone knows you can't be too picky after 35. So even though I used to hope for a smart, successful, charming guy, now I'll just set my sights on a dumb, unmotivated, boring guy.* Sure, that makes sense.

But single women aren't the only ones who field such comments. In fact, anyone remotely connected to us should take heed. As I noted earlier, my poor mother got this little zinger, too. "Karin hasn't found anyone yet? Maybe she's being too picky..." Nice to know my lingering single status garnered insults for both me *and* my mother. Knowing that women can be catty at any age (see Chapter 2), I have to wonder what's behind the "Your daughter's too picky" remarks mothers receive:

- I guess your daughter isn't quite the catch she thinks she is. She better go ahead and settle for whomever will give her a second look.

- Your daughter acts like she's hot stuff, but her arrogance makes her unattractive. Men don't go for women like that.

- You raised a little spoiled princess. Now look at the mess you have on your hands.

- Your snotty daughter thinks she's too good for anyone. It serves her right she's still single. Ha!

Okay, maybe there's no "Ha!" involved...

PSYCH 101: WHY THEY DO IT

Honestly, I don't understand why anyone would encourage a woman to be less selective when choosing the person with whom she plans to spend the rest of her life. It seems like a pretty rotten idea all the way around. But let's assume most people have good intentions and are sincerely trying to help us. If that's the case, what might motivate the "you're too picky" comments?

In general, I imagine the "picky" slurs come from people who operate from a vastly different position than us. For instance, some women connect well with a wide array of men; they don't really have a "type". They love 'em all—jocks, hipsters, surfers, suits, artists, nerds, sugar daddies, and boy toys. But perhaps you're the exact opposite. You know what works for you and don't want to waste time dating a homebody when your wanderlust will inevitably drive him nuts. Friends with a more equal-opportunity approach to dating might wonder why you pass up offers from decent guys. And because they're a bit more flexible in their selection process, they perceive you as picky.

Others might claim you're too picky because they're fixated on marriage. Those in this camp believe a woman hasn't "arrived" until she's donned the title of wife. Unable to comprehend an existence *sans* husband, they care little about whom we marry, just so long as we marry. To them, all guys are about the same anyway; just grab one and go with it. And perhaps they weren't all that picky themselves, so what's our problem?

Similarly, some women push marriage for the purpose of procreation. They *must* get married because they *must* be mommies. Reproduction is the ultimate goal and they intend to make it happen. No question. Therefore, when dating, this type of woman sizes up a guy primarily on his fathering potential.

49

This quality might prove even more important than the romantic chemistry she has with her partner or how well they click as a couple. How she feels about her boyfriend holds less weight than how eager he is to hold babies at her family reunion. Such women won't understand you're looking for more than just a baby daddy. They don't get it. So to them, you're just being too picky.

And by the way, that's fine—for them. No judgment for marrying whatever man for whatever reason. If a good-enough guy who'll provide a good-enough life is good enough, great! If he's got good-enough genes to make good-enough babies—good-enough! But, if you want a husband who's your best friend, best lover, and best partner, then by all means, be PICKY!

Finally, and this is a depressing one, but I suppose it's conceivable that, in some instances, people call you picky because down deep they feel they settled and they hate watching you hold out for the right one. I hope this isn't the case, but the possibility exists.

It just hasn't happened yet

Okay, for the sake of argument, let's pretend to ignore this chapter and admit to ourselves our friends are right. We plead guilty and promise to knock it off.

What, exactly, might happen if single women stopped being so darn picky?

Well, if we go with the mindset that all guys are about the same and just take any old one, we'll probably find ourselves in lackluster marriages. Aiming the bar so low may cause us to feel superior to our spouses, introducing a dynamic of inequity into the relationship. That's always good for marriages, right? Best-case scenario, we pity our husbands. Worst-case scenario? We despise them and despise ourselves for settling.

Or, if the kid factor wins out, we might embark upon a marriage of convenience—partners in parenting, but nothing else. Since our marriage is all about the children, we might as well forget about romance and select someone who'll be a good father and a good pal.

And what about those children we so desperately desired? They get to witness a loveless union—what a wonderful example to set for them! Best case scenario? Years of quiet desperation. Worst case scenario? Extra-marital affairs, divorce, and a nasty custody battle. (Again, great familial baggage to dump on our kids.) But at least we're mommies.

Furthermore, our fantasy of a home full of rosy-faced, happy cherubs has little chance of materializing because if we settle for a mediocre marriage, our kids will more than likely grow up severely troubled.

In fact, family therapists assert that children react behaviorally to turbulence and unhappiness in their parents' marriage *i.e.* when spouses' lack a deep, intimate connection or exhibit hostility toward each other, children pick up on it and act out in myriad negative ways. Furthermore, many psychologists believe the vast majority of children labeled as ADHD and bipolar are misdiagnosed. These kids endure the brunt of their parents' dysfunctional relationship by being diagnosed as mentally ill when in actuality, they're merely unwittingly responding to unhealthy family dynamics. On a positive note, most kids with such labels can improve dramatically and be taken off medication after just a few sessions of family therapy.[6]

Putting aside the family fallout, how cruel is it to even consider marrying (or dating) a guy who thinks you're madly in love with him, who thinks he's the man of your dreams, when, actually, the only reason you're with him is that you *lowered* your standards! Best-case scenario? He lives a lie for 50 years. Worst-case scenario? He eventually realizes you never truly had it for him and leaves you for someone who will honestly love him. Or maybe that *is* the best case scenario...

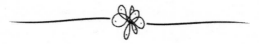

Ditto

Right. We get it. We're super-picky, super-spoiled, stuck-up little princesses, fully deserving of derision and disdain.

Or maybe, just maybe, we're not complete and utter snobs, but rather, responsible women doing the right thing by waiting for the right one. Leslie Talbot, author of *It's Better To Be Single Than To Wish You Were*, supports this perspective.

"As one of our nation's 90 million unmarried citizens, I've become inured to the social pressure to couple up—the backhanded insults and armchair psychoanalysis meted out by friends, co-workers, and well-meaning strangers at the bus stop whenever my marital status comes under scrutiny. And, believe me, I've heard it all. Selfish? Check. Immature? Check. Emotionally unstable? Check. Too picky for my own good? Check, check, and check.

But I've never bought into the prevailing notion that a perfectly fulfilling singular existence is little more than a karmic consolation prize. As far as I'm concerned, there's no more *un*fulfilling existence than one spent trapped with the wrong person. Take my word for it—a loveless marriage will sap your spirit and your sanity a lot more quickly than a lifetime of dateless Saturday nights. For me, then, and for many of the adults in this country who are single, singlehood is not merely the right choice. It is the responsible choice."[7]

Girl Talk

Dear Karin,

I hate to break it to ya, but this chapter wasn't helpful at all. I used to be irritated when people told me I was too picky. Now I'm full-on offended! Thanks a lot!

But I do hear it all the time. My aunt tells me I'm too picky. My sister says the same thing. So do the women at work. And you're right—our mothers get it, too. My mom told me her best friend never shuts up about how picky I am. Between you and me, though, I think she's just bitter because a few years ago she set me up on a date with her son, Jake. We went out a couple times and he was a great guy—attractive, smart funny, and successful. But I just wasn't feelin' it, which was really too bad because he's a catch! Anyway, my mom's best friend has had an attitude with me ever since. And I guess in her head, I'm too picky because I wasn't into her kid.

But to be honest, sometimes I do second guess myself. I wonder if I'm holding out for some ideal man who doesn't exist. I mean, what if I'm being unrealistic

waiting for the fantasy of the perfect guy? A Prince Charming who looks like George Clooney but with Bono's bleeding heart, Bill Gates' brains, and Donald Trump's business acumen? Am I kidding myself?
— *Courtney, 28*

Dear Courtney,

First of all, when you meet that Prince Charming, please let me know if he's open to being cloned because every single woman I know would go crazy for your Clooney/Bono/Gates/Trump hybrid.

But to answer your question, are you kidding yourself? I don't think so. Look at it this way. You said yourself that Jake was a great guy and you *wish* you could have fallen for him because he would have given you a fantastic life. But I'm willing to bet that you *have* fallen for some guys in the past who weren't even the "catch" Jake was—guys who, on paper, pale in comparison to Jake but who "did it" for you, guys with whom you had, for whatever reason, that indescribable chemistry and spark. After all, there's an element to attraction that can't be quantified. We can't put our finger on it, but we know it when we feel it. And we know when we *don't* feel it.

So give yourself a break. I doubt you're holding out for an unrealistic Prince Charming. But you are waiting for *your* Prince Charming. He may look more like Bill Gates than George Clooney (dang it!). He might have Bono's business savvy (well, he's pretty shrewd) with Donald Trump's hair (but really, that's got to be a toupée, right?). The point is, you'll fall in love because of your connection and chemistry. And any imperfections he has won't even faze you, because he's the one for you. Those deficits may have bothered other women he dated. Maybe they even broke up with him for those same flaws. But of course, they were being way too picky.

— Karin

The Awful Truth

Remember, these scenes are not *based* on real stories. They *are* real stories!

BEGGARS CAN'T BE CHOOSERS

CAST.
TRICIA: single 33-year-old school social worker
STEPHANIE: single 28-year-old 5th grade
    teacher
MARY PAT: smug teacher married for 15 years
    to "my husband, the lawyer"

INTERIOR — BAR/GRILL — NIGHT

MARY PAT
So, ladies, how 'bout that waiter for one of you guys? He's a cutie.

TRICIA
Mary Pat, he's like 21!

MARY PAT
Well, maybe you're too old for him, Tricia, but Stephanie might be interested.

TRICIA
Steph, Mary Pat's decided I'm a dried up spinster and way too old for the waiter, but you could give it a shot. Whaddya think?

STEPHANIE
The waiter? Are you kidding me? He's *obviously* gay.

MARY PAT
Ugh! No wonder you girls are still single. You're way too picky!

Lesson Learned: If you're in your 30s and still single, it's time to consider gay guys. Hoping for a heterosexual constitutes being too picky.

Guy Talk

Seriously, from a guy's perspective, Karin is right on the money. I know women think men are the cruel ones, but we actually get our little hearts broken every once in a while. It's rough out there for us, too. And the last thing we need is to start going out with some hot chick (who we kinda think is way out of our league, anyway) just to find out she's experimenting with being less picky about her dates and we're the lucky guinea pig. That's really uncool.

And I know what you're thinking: "Well, if I date down for a couple weeks, at least I've done a good deed. I've given some poor fool a moment of bliss with my goddess self." Look, that's no consolation. Leave us poor fools alone! That little moment with your goddess self could ruin us. Even if we only date you for a few weeks, we'll start thinking we can hang with your crowd. We'll be convinced we can play in the big leagues. We'll believe we're destined to date super-models all the time and we won't be satisfied with women we actually *can* date. So please, ladies, have a heart! Be picky!

— Guy

Wow. See why we need a guy's point of view? I would've never thought of any of that. But there you have it. Apparently, it's not cruel to be picky; it's cruel to *not* be picky. I love it!

— Karin

Selfie

Sometimes, when you constantly hear how picky you are, you start believing it.

When Kyle (my college boyfriend) and I finally broke up for good in my mid-twenties, I reluctantly entered the singles' scene. Although our relationship had never felt 100% right, I'd held out hope that our circuitous path would straighten out once I got my act together—finished grad school, became more independent from my parents, and "found myself". But after our demise, I was, for the first time in my adult life, completely without a boyfriend.

For the latter part of my twenties, I dated here and there, but kept Kyle on a pedestal and, to my mind, no one compared to him and the intense connection we had. Disinclined to move on and still pining for him, I drove everyone around me pretty crazy. My parents couldn't understand why I remained so fixated on Kyle, insisting there were plenty of men much better suited for me. Friends called me picky and got irritated with me for refusing to give new guys a chance.

And I completely agreed with them, by the way. I felt like a disappointing daughter, annoying friend, and train wreck of a romantic partner. How did I get here? This was *not* the plan!

So on my 30th birthday when I met a smart, successful, kind-hearted guy, I told myself that although he wasn't my type, my expectations were probably completely unrealistic. When he asked for my number, I gave it to him.

Three years later, he proposed and I accepted.

Had he grown on me? Yes. Did I respect and care for him? Of course. Was I in love with him? Not at all. But at 33, I couldn't afford to be too picky.

More to come on this story...

Shout Out!

So to my smart, sexy, savvy, singletons I say this: If someone tells you you're too picky, agree with them! Of course you're selective! Settling for anything less than an extraordinary relationship is not an option! And until one comes along, you'll be just fine... because single is the new black!

chapter 4

It's Not Because You Need to Get Back "Out There"!

rumor has it the "Land of Out There" is ripe with available men. . .

I'm tired of getting "out there". It hasn't done any good. Where I live it's hard to meet good guys anyhow. So I just quit every time.
— Leah, 34

Okay, first of all, you *are* out there. Unless, of course, you spend your days sequestered off from society, curled up in the fetal position, rocking back and forth, chanting a *get-a-man-tra* of "Someday my prince will come." Please! The single women I know *are* out there. Where else would they be?

Nevertheless I *know* you've heard this one. Getting back "out there" may be the most commonly provided explanation for why the unattached aren't dating. It's a particular favorite of happy couples, especially those who've been married for so many years they hardly remember being single. Smugly snuggled up in their suburban great rooms, they sip Diet Cokes and ponder the fate of their pitiful unmarried friends. "I can't believe Christa is still single! Why can't she meet a nice guy? There's got to be something she could do to meet desirable men!" They put their heads together, determined to ascertain an action plan to assist their solitary friend. Then, in a flash of insight, it comes to them. So simple, yet so profound. So brilliant, yet so facile. They can't wait to share the epiphany with their poor, lonely-hearted girlfriend! *She just needs to...* (drum roll, please)... get back *"Out There"*.

How charming, too, that those who give us the get back "out there" pep talks are frequently people who never had to extend themselves whatsoever when trying to connect with the opposite sex. Their spouses simply fell into their laps. They met in graduate school or at the health club or in the waiting room at the dentist or at work or standing in line at the bank.

So just where, exactly, do our married friends imagine we are all day? And just what, exactly, do they think we're doing? From my observations, most single women engage in many of the same activities that brought love to their friends—they're attending graduate courses, working out at health clubs, sitting in waiting rooms at dentists' offices, going to work, and standing in line at the bank. But we haven't met him yet. So does that mean we need to get "out there" *more*?

And we do—to get "out there" *more*, we plan ladies' nights, don sexy little sandals and skimpy little skirts and hit the town. We make concerted efforts to see and be seen at the swankiest restaurants and hottest clubs. Sometimes we meet men. Sometimes we don't. And when we strike out, then what? All those big attempts to get "out there" *more* didn't work, so now what are we supposed to do? Have we not extended ourselves enough already? Apparently not.

So we hurl ourselves out further and further, exploring more-creative options—speed dating, First Fridays, cooking classes, wine tastings, theater openings, charity benefits, and singles' cruises. The "out there" fever consumes us as a frenzied momentum builds. *Maybe my friends are right! Getting "out there" is gonna get me a man!* So thoroughly brainwashed by this balderdash, we sometimes even feel guilty for occasionally wanting to stay home for an evening. *I'm so tired from working all week. All I want to do is soak in the tub. But this could be the night I meet him! I'd never forgive myself for missing out on Mr. Wonderful just because I was too lazy to glam up and go out on a Friday night. Everyone says I need to get "out there"...*

PSYCH 101: WHY THEY DO IT

This one goes back to the ever-present culprit—control. Your friends see that you're lonely sometimes. They know you get tired of going stag to weddings. They hear your horror stories and feel your pain. And as much as your peeps love you, they can't do a darn thing about it. If they could wave a magic wand and summon Mr. Right, they would in a second. But they can't. And they feel bad for you, which makes *them* feel bad.

And no one wants to feel bad 'cause that's no fun. So instead of sitting with the discomfort and admitting it stinks, they try to figure it all out. Swell idea, but what's to be done with circumstances completely out of their control? Nothing—except, of course, to tell you to get "out there". They comfort themselves thinking this sagacious suggestion will somehow solve your dilemma. Whew! Now they can feel better because they've given you the best advice they have.

As an added bonus, it kind of takes them off the hook. Because if you don't get "out there" enough (*enough* being whatever subjective standard they've set), they won't have to feel sorry for you anymore—"I told her to get 'out there' more, but she doesn't! What's the matter with her?" Pity morphs into blame because you're clearly responsible for your solitary state. You're just not getting "out there" enough!

None of this is intentional, of course. Your friends don't ever say to themselves, "It pains me to see Britney all alone. I know she hasn't had a boyfriend in a while and she'd like to be dating someone. She's hurting and that makes me feel bad. Hmm. I sure don't want to feel bad... I know what I'll do! I'll give her a lame idea to get 'out there'! That way, I've done my part. And if she doesn't take me up on my advice, well then, that's on her. Done and done! I sure hope this works, because I'd really like to stop feeling sorry about her lack of a love life."

It just hasn't happened yet

Well, as noted previously, someone's got to take the blame for your single status, right? And once again, you're the fall guy (well, fall girl). If you'd only position yourself more effectively and truly commit to finding a man, it would happen. Use a little strategy, for goodness' sake! Launch yourself into every conceivable male milieu. Perform daily operations in husband hunting. Get serious about the pursuit and it will all work out.

Once again, you get the message you're doing something wrong. It's your fault you're single. If you'd just get off your tush and make an effort, you'd meet him. It's time to get intentional about this, darn it! Get back "out there"!

Nice. It sure feels good to get blamed for something you already feel cruddy about but can't change. In their attempts to help, friends end up making things worse. Sure it's unintentional, but that's what happens.

Ditto

Sociologist E. Kay Trimberger's research challenges the effectiveness of strategies like getting "out there". For over twenty years, Trimberger has studied unmarried women, chronicling the vicissitudes of navigating single life in a couples' world. Her participants represent the gamut—women who have made peace with their status and those who continue to pursue marriage.

Trimberger notes that a relentless quest for coupledom may be related to a reduction in life satisfaction. Through observations and interviews, she has found that those single women who put the *most* energy and effort into trying to find a partner appear to be the *least* happy.[8]

So, although offered with the best of intentions, those "you just need to get back out there" pep talks from your friends and family might be the least helpful suggestion they could give.

Girl Talk

Dear Karin,

Oh my gosh! If I had a quarter for every time one of my happily married friends has given me the "You gotta get out there" pitch, I'd be a millionaire! I just wanna smack 'em!

Take my friend, Lauren. She's the worst offender—especially since she has absolutely no idea what she's talking about. She serial-dated throughout college and then landed a fluff job as a receptionist at a law firm. Within a month she began seeing this young, hotshot attorney. Six weeks later, she moved in with him. Fast forward four years, and they're married.

The best part is, she constantly reminisces about her lonely post-college single days, and she acts like she's <u>finally</u> settling down after years of tearing up the town with her Holly Golightly self. But it's not like you're really single if you have a serious boyfriend and you live with him! Give me a break!

But, like I said, she's the one who preaches the "out there" message non-stop. It's always, "Jill, you're never going to meet a man if you only hang out at gay bars singing show-tune karaoke! I know you pride yourself on being a fruit fly, but flitting around with fairies won't get you a husband! You gotta get where the action is. You know what you should do? Check out some of the bars downtown where the traders go for happy hour..."

As if she knows the first thing about being single! All she did was show up to work one day and score herself a junior partner. Did she have to get "out there" to meet her man? I don't think so.

Am I wrong to be a little bitter?

— Jill, 32

Dear Jill,

I don't hear bitterness—I hear you stating the facts. What's most irritating about Lauren is that she thinks she's an expert on what you're going through when, clearly, she has no clue. If she did, she'd realize just how insensitive she is with her "out there" solution. All the single women I know *hate* when people tell them this. So, you've got a point—she was never really single. At least not single the way you're single.

And by the way, gay bars are a single girl's best friend! What's better than a room full of beautiful boys, who can actually sing karaoke and who talk to you without looking you up and down, unless it's to compliment you on your fashion-forward ensemble. They never approach you with tacky pick-up lines, and they love dishing on all the same stuff you do—pop culture, celebrity gossip, and interior design. Plus, at least one of them will have the word on which stylists do the best highlights—and that's *priceless* information.

At a gay bar you can totally be yourself because no one ever mistakes your friendliness for flirtation; no mess, no fuss, no confusion (except for when the bisexuals show up and throw us all off, but that's another story). Again, if Lauren had actually been single for a while, she would know the haven that is the gay bar and the joy of "straight-girl/gay-boy" love.

— Karin

The Awful Truth

Remember, these scenes are not *based* on real stories. They *are* real stories!

DOUBLE BIND

CAST.
KATE: single, 25-year-old graduate student
BARB: her mother

INTERIOR — KATE'S CITY APARTMENT — DAY

Kate is on the phone with her mother, who lives in a nearby suburb.

BARB

So, honey, do you have any good news for me?

                    KATE

Mom, if you're referring to my
love life, then, no, I suppose I
don't.

                    BARB

[sighs] Well, I guess I really
shouldn't expect any new
developments since you're making
absolutely no effort to meet
anyone!

                    KATE

[exasperated] Unbelievable! You
think I'm not trying?

                    BARB

No, I certainly don't think you're
trying. I don't see you doing
anything at all to meet men. I've
told you before, you've got to
extend yourself a bit, Kate. Get
back "out there"! Guys aren't
going to just come knocking on
your door!

                    KATE

For your information, Mom, I AM
extending myself. Do you want
details? Let me break it down for

you—in the last couple weeks I've joined two match making websites, attended a speed-dating event, went to a singles' cooking class and signed up to play co-ed softball through the Chicago Social Network.

BARB

You mean to tell me you've done all that and you haven't met even one nice boy?

KATE

Yes, Mom. That's exactly what I'm telling you.

BARB

Oh, for heaven's sake, Kate. If that's the case then you must be doing something wrong. You're probably coming across as way too desperate!

Kate slams down the phone.

Lesson Learned: It's *always* your fault. *Always!* If you heed the "get back out there" mandate without success, then obviously you messed it up. You got out *too* far

71

or got lost and ended up in the wrong *there*. Or you're acting too desperate. Or something.

Guy Talk

"Out there", huh? Is that where we guys are supposed to be? I'm gonna assume you're looking for a dude like me, which might be a stretch, I know, but I'm here to give the guys' perspective so... And I don't know where I am exactly, but I can definitely say I'm not "out there" and neither are my guy friends. We're just living our lives and doing our thing. We're going to the dentist and the bank and all those other places Karin said single women go. Although I haven't seen a hot chick at the dentist since I was 12 when I had this huge crush on the hygienist at my orthodontist's office. Wait, does that count? I used to eat popcorn on purpose just to try to break my braces so my mom would have to schedule appointments... (Um, could ya get back to the point? — Karin) Right, the point is, I can't tell you exactly where to go to meet us, but we're around and we're looking. In fact, a lot of us are just like you; we're keeping an eye open for a love connection if one should happen to walk by.

But as for the gay bars? Karin's way off here. First of all, Lauren is right. Straight guys *don't* go to gay bars, so Jill will never meet potential marriage material there. Secondly, "fruit flies" (is that the new PC term?) are a total turn off to straight men. It's way too intimidating to date a woman with a lot of gay friends. I mean, how can we compete with those guys—they're good listeners! They actually *enjoy* all the foolish minutiae women bore us with when telling a story! Plus, they rarely audibly belch! And they send cards and flowers for birthdays and anniversaries whereas straight men are lucky if they even *remember* the dates in the first place. They spoil their "girlfriends" and all this does is ruin it for straight guys 'cause women start becoming accustomed to all this attention.

I dated a "fruit fly" once and it was a nightmare. She constantly compared me to all her "gay boyfriends", and of course, I always came up short. No, I won't wear skin tight designer jeans. No, I don't want to peruse last week's issue of *People*. And for the love of Pete, turn off the HGTV!

— Guy

Well, obviously we part ways on this one. I recognize that the natural affinity between gay men and straight women rarely translates to gay men and straight men, but what's with the hostility? Can't we all just get along?

— Karin

Selfie

If they'd ever crowned a Queen of Out There, I'd have earned the title.

What other choice did I have? I wanted to find love so I did what we all do. I joined social groups, sports teams, gyms, clubs, and organizations. I went to parties, street fests, parks, libraries, and museums. I tried speed and online dating. I attended mixers, concerts, and charity benefits. I met lots of guys and went on loads of dates. And after every failed relationship, I picked myself up, dusted myself off, and got back *out there*.

But getting *out there* can take its toll. One time during a particularly long dry spell, I orchestrated a girls' night. Determined to wrench my friends and I out of our dating slumps, I decided we should check out a hot new club in trendy Lincoln Park. Working the room, we danced for hours, chatting up guy after guy, yet none of us connected with even one eligible gentleman.

"No worries, ladies! Let's just head to the next spot!" Again, no luck.

Pressing on to still another bar, we continued to hold out hope but to no avail.

Now utterly demoralized, I finally threw in the towel. Three different clubs. Hundreds of perfectly nice, attractive, charming guys. Four adorable women, if I do say so myself. What was the problem? This whole getting out there thing is exhausting and painful! Ugh!

And just to be clear, I hadn't expected to find the love of my life on that random Saturday night; that would have been shooting for the stars. All I really wanted was to perhaps meet someone halfway decent who I could talk to and with whom I had even a little chemistry, someone who'd give me hope that The One might still be out there. But it wasn't happening that night. And sadly, a lot of my "I gotta get out there" efforts ended in the exact same way leaving me dejected, deflated, and defeated.

So much for getting back out there!

Shout Out!

So to my smart, sexy, savvy, singletons I say this: I know you're "out there"! You know you're "out there"! We all know you're "out there"! So obviously, that's not the issue. People who say this to you just don't get it. You know why you're still single? Because it just hasn't happened yet. And that's perfectly fine... because single is the new black!

chapter 5

It's Not Because
You Need to
"Tone It Down a Notch"!

um, are we living in 1895?

What strikes me about all the advice we get, especially the pat phrases, is how anti-feminist it is. What they're really saying is, "You're not acting in a feminine enough way. Be prettier! Be more passive! Don't be so much yourself; only demure girls get men—and you're nothing if you don't have a man." Meanwhile, everything I've read from the gripe tripe of pop psych to more meaty scientific articles suggests that single women suffer far less than single men. They tend to need us a lot more than we need them. I think women are pressured to attach themselves to men partly because of that and partly because having a male partner is seen as a sign of social accomplishment. It's not really about what a woman needs emotionally.

— Anne, 38

You've come a long way, baby! Be anything! Be everything! You can have it all! Stretch, grow, excel, shine! Nothing's holding you back! Reach for the stars! Play among the stars! *Be* a star!

At least, that's what they told us when we were little.

So we did. Lived our lives to the fullest, exceeded our potential in every area, all the while basking in the praise of friends and family cheering from the sidelines: "Look at her go!" "So ambitious! So accomplished!" "We couldn't be prouder!"

And they were—proud of us, that is. Until we ran into some trouble achieving the most critical and crucial of womanly pursuits—the hunt for a husband. Then they changed their tune:

- "Hmmm... Still single at 30. I wonder if you intimidate men."

- "Well, you're pretty opinionated. A lot of guys might find that to be a bit much."

- "Of course, you do have a lot of degrees. Most men don't want a wife who's more educated than they are."

- "You know, men marry down and women marry up. You've worked yourself into a

> situation where there aren't too many men
> left in the tiers above you."

- "I'm not saying you should 'dumb it
  down' or anything, but maybe rein things
  in a bit so guys won't feel so threatened by
  you."

So after years of profuse encouragement to
reach, soar, strive, and achieve, now we hear we need to
"tone it down a notch". Seriously?

Oh yeah, they're serious. And we better get
with the program if we think we're ever going to find
our way to the altar. Wake up, ladies! All that girl
power flies at sorority conventions and book clubs, but
we better keep it under wraps when in the company of
eligible bachelors—at least if we hope to appeal to said
eligibles. Because, apparently, over the last 50 years as
women gained equality, men missed the memo.

Well, okay, to be fair, some men got the memo,
and indisputably the social climate in the latter part of
the twentieth century ignited profound changes for
both sexes. Gender expectations relaxed and women
began to revel in myriad opportunities—so much so
that currently more women complete college than men.
And in many graduate programs and professions,
females lead the way. Gone is the time when the apex
of a woman's existence consisted of squeezing into a

torpedo bra, whipping up fondue in high heels, and washing down an insipid, identity-stifling suburban-housewife life with "mother's little helpers".

So, clearly, we represent liberated women of the 21st century, right? Our generation escaped the confines of female role-entrapment. The gender revolution of the 1960s and 1970s brought forth a new day, providing women with infinite opportunities and the freedom to pursue their true, genuine selves. The women's movement hit, and all the sexist rules got thrown out the window. Or so we thought.

PSYCH 101: WHY THEY DO IT

Apparently, some of those rules fell a few feet shy of the window and got neatly swept under the rug. Now surreptitiously out of sight, they remain, arguably, more powerful and difficult to tackle in their covert state. And the most persistent of these dictates? The ones pressuring us to partner. Because no matter how successful and accomplished and brilliant a woman is, she's still a failure without a man. Period.

No one admits it outright—that would be so last millennium—but subverted, biased ideation clutches white-knuckled to our collective consciousness, so cleverly that we often remain oblivious to our own bigoted positions—until the sneaky sexism comes up for air, outing itself in directives such as "Tone it down a notch" or "Be careful! Don't intimidate men or you'll never get one."

Often, however, it manifests more subtly, creeping circuitously into our explanations of relationship demise: "Well, they were both up-and-coming attorneys, but she eventually made partner and he didn't. If you ask me, it took a huge toll on them. That's when things turned south." Or, "You know, she had a slew of boyfriends in college, but she's very driven. And how many men want a wife who works 12 hour days?" Or, "Sure, she's ambitious and attractive, but Jim's not the kind of guy who planned on competing with his wife's career—or with his wife!" Or, "She's so quick-witted and super smart. You could tell it bothered him; he felt upstaged all the time."

Sadly, these scoldings come not only from those with "old school" ideology, but also from peers and contemporaries—our "girls". Sexism is alive and well, concealed from view, but still wielding its potency.

Naturally, those who tell us to "tone it down" are just trying to help. And obviously, they fail to think through their reasoning before spewing such inane counsel. If people actually reflected for a moment, could they possibly believe anyone benefits from one member of a relationship essentially faking it by presenting a watered-down version of herself?

Ditto

A clear expression of the "tone it down" sentiment surfaced as a cautionary statistic in the infamous 1986 *Newsweek* article which declared a single, 40-year-old college educated woman was more likely to be killed by a terrorist than ever get married.

Twenty years later when *Newsweek* admitted the inaccuracy of the data, many writers like Kira Cochrane responded strongly: "Let's face it, this notion, with its brilliant conjunction of loneliness and violent death, always seemed pretty suspect. Nonetheless, the statistic gained stunning popularity. As the perfect, doom-laden warning to all us pesky women who insist on, you know, enjoying ourselves, getting educated and developing a career before settling down, it has become one of the most repeated statistics of all time. [If you] spotted a single thirty-something woman having fun? Just warn her that she has more chance of being bombed than getting anyone to love her and commit to her. That'll wipe the smile off her face!"[9]

Writer Lynn Harris also spoke to the *Newsweek* retraction, focusing on "one of the 14 then-doomed singles interviewed in 1986. Guess what? She got married at 40 and remains blissfully so at 50. 'I've watched a lot of people [who married while young] get divorced,' she says. 'I think that if you do wait until Mr. Right comes along, you have a much better chance of survival.'"[10]

So how about some valid research on the subject? Economist Heather Boushy analyzed U.S. survey data of over 33 million women and found that high achieving women are no less likely than average working women to be married or have children by age 40.[11]

Another study by sociologist Christine Whalen resulted in even more promising findings. Whalen reports that in the age bracket of 30 to 44, women who earn over $100,000 a year are *more* likely to be married than women earning less.[12]

Apparently, all those career women making six figures didn't "tone it down a notch" and look what happened—they got it all!

It just hasn't happened yet

No question—though we live in a post-feminism era, residual, archaic conceptions of women's value and worth persist. So where does that leave us?

If we made the "mistake" of believing we should reach our fullest potential and we did, in fact, accomplish, acquire, and achieve, we may now learn we've painted ourselves into a mate-finding corner, albeit an impressive and remarkable corner, but a corner nonetheless. So "up" we have nowhere to go but "down". Our choices? Take their advice and rein ourselves in a bit or carry a mantle of "To thine own self be true" and search for partners without a whole lot going for them. Wow. Both options sound so very enticing.

But what's even more troubling to me is our response. They warn us to "tone it down" and sometimes, in our weaker moments, we actually consider it. We crack. We cave. We concede and wonder if they've got a point. Why? Because we, too, fail to appreciate the power of these unseen, antiquated notions pressing upon our psyches and asserting their influence, causing us to doubt and question our very selves. Supposedly, we've come a long way, baby. Yeah, right.

Girl Talk

Dear Karin,

"Tone it down a notch" is the worst! Whenever I hear it I always get furious at the idiot who had the nerve to say it. If repressing a part of who I am is what it takes to get a guy, then I'm happy to write off marriage all together. I want a husband who can keep up with me, not drag me down, and I have no intentions of settling. The sky's the limit, and I can take care of myself!

But here's what I want to know. Do men ever get this garbage? I mean, if a guy is 35 and single, do his family members pull him aside at Christmas parties and suggest that the reason he can't find a girlfriend is because he's just a bit "too much" for women to handle? Do they make him doubt his great, gutsy qualities or encourage him to be anything less than who he is? Of course not! It's appalling that people feel perfectly comfortable saying such offensive things to women that I know for a fact they'd never utter to a man. What's that all about, anyway?

Someone once told me that American women are the most liberated in the world. I'm kinda doubting it.

— Alex, 27

Dear Alex,

I agree. No argument here. Do guys get this stuff? Definitely not! They've certainly got their own junk to deal with (and I'm sure Guy will clue us in on it shortly) but it's not the same. And if you ask me, we get it way worse. Maybe I'm not being sensitive enough to guys' experiences but, hey, some dude can write a book for them.

— Karin

The Awful Truth

Remember, these scenes are not *based* on real stories. They *are* real stories!

TOO MUCH IS NEVER ENOUGH

CAST.
ANGELA: single 38-year-old college professor
MONA: Angela's aunt, whom she rarely sees
LOIS: married 37-year-old stay-at-home-mom.
    Angela's cousin and Mona's daughter

EXTERIOR — COMMUNITY PARK — DAY

The family is gathering for its annual reunion. Angela is home for the first time in several years. Angela, Mona, and Lois stand together eating brownies.

> MONA
>
> [to Lois] Now would you look at Angela? Is she a catch or what? I can't imagine why she's not taken! What are those men missing? Can't they see it?

> LOIS
>
> [embarrassed] Please, Mom, what are you talking about? Of course

men see it! I'm sure Angela is just
being   discriminating—as   she
should be!

                    MONA
[to Angela] No seriously, how is it
that a man hasn't snatched you
up?

Angela laughs uncomfortably.

                    ANGELA
Oh, you know, Aunt Mona. I just
keep flitting away! They can't pin
me down!

Mona's eyes widen and she nods with
understanding.

                    MONA
Of course! That's it! You're just
too much for them! So brilliant!
So talented! So beautiful! They
wouldn't even know what to do
with you. Really, I'm sure most
men just can't keep up!

                    ANGELA
Well, I don't know about that...

MONA

And we all know how men are.
They've got to feel like they're in
charge and they certainly wouldn't
with you. I get it now, like I said,
you're just too much for them.

LOIS

Great, Mom. Real encouraging.

MONA

Well, sure it's encouraging! Now
we understand what the problem
is.

LOIS

I'm not sure anyone thought there
was a problem in the first place,
Mom! Could you just leave her
alone already?

Angela quietly makes an escape while Lois and
Mona's arguing escalates.

Lesson Learned: If you're perceived as a "catch" but
haven't been "caught" people may formulate
explanations concerning the *immensity* of you. I'm not
quite sure if this speaks to your personality, intellect,
abilities, accomplishments, presence, aura, emanations,
subtle body or what. But somehow, in some way,

you're just too much! You're so great and it's making everyone else feel bad, especially the guys, so can't you tone it down a notch already?

Guy Talk

My only reaction to this chapter is a resounding, *Huh?* I mean, Karin makes a strong case for the reasons behind this kind of lame advice, but I still don't get it.

For one thing, I can't figure out what exactly you women are supposed to "tone down". And I'm totally clueless about this business of being "too much" or "too threatening" because the vast majority of guys I know love spunky women. As a matter of fact, I hear way more complaints from my friends about girls being passive and boring. You know the whole, "Where do you want to go for dinner tonight?" And all he ever hears is, "I don't care. You pick." Now *that* will drive a man crazy. But a woman with a brain and some attitude? Please, the guys are gonna be all over her. Don't you know men love nothing more than a challenge?

Oh, and while we're on the subject, lean in and listen closely. Guys HATE when women are phony. We despise it in every way, shape or form, except for a small subset of us who like the phony things that result from certain surgical procedures, if you know what I mean. (Seriously, Guy? — Karin) Hey, I said it was a minority of us...

Anyway, I can tell you for a fact that I've heard plenty of talk over beer and brats about how this or that chick plays games and is full of crap and is never straight-up about anything. Trust me. By the end of that conversation, every guy at the table detests that girl.

So, I gotta say, I think "toning it down" is probably some of the worst advice a woman could get. It would most likely backfire because if a guy senses that a woman is trying to be anything other than herself, he's gonna bolt. No questions asked.

— Guy

Veni. Vidi. Vici.

— Karin

Selfie

This topic is so absurd to me I almost didn't include it in the book.

However, after multiple interviews with single women, I realized I couldn't ignore it if I wanted to accurately represent the experiences of my readers and the inane comments they incessantly field.

In fact, one dating/relationship writer I spoke with pretty much begged me to devote a chapter to this subject because, as she put it, "All my single friends hear this message in one way, shape, or form. And for me personally, it's absolutely the most offensive thing someone could say. You've *got to* tackle it!" So although I wanted to dismiss the ludicrous warning and its appalling implications, I had to address it. Hence, the chapter.

Not that I'd been exempt from such admonition. Over my 20+ years of single adulthood, I heard plenty of voices imparting similar thoughts. When I started my Ph.D. program, for example, I received several not-so-subtle warnings that highly educated women intimidate men. And from time to time, in order to account for my enduring singleness, a friend would wonder if perhaps I were a bit too outspoken with my theories and viewpoints because apparently, though we live in the 21st century, opinionated women still threaten men.

But ultimately, the "tone it down a notch" warning never took root with me. How could it? I knew too many brilliant, assertive, vociferous women— women who were way sassier than me, and much more prone to toss out compelling arguments in mixed company on any issue *du jour.* Yet low and behold, these women were married! Somehow, someway, my smart, successful friends had remained 100% themselves and still managed to snag husbands who loved them— brains, opinions, swagger, and all. So I figured, if they could find true love without toning it down a notch, I probably could, too.

Shout Out!

So to my smart, sexy, savvy singletons I say this: You better not tone down even one tiny ounce of your fantastic self. Your future husband would be so disappointed if you did! Stay authentically you because someone wants exactly what you have to offer. It's your time to shine... because single is the new black.

chapter 6

It's Not Because You're Not Trying Hard Enough!

so don't feel obligated to go on every blind date that's thrown your way

Being single while almost everybody else is married can sometimes be a little tough, especially when all your married friends try to pair you up with anybody they believe would be a good partner. What's stressful is when you don't feel like going out with the guy and they feel you're being too picky. I get mad, but then I think, "If I don't try harder I might be alone forever!" But is love supposed to feel like pulling teeth or running a marathon?

— Denise, 32

"You're not trying hard enough." I wish I could chalk up this criticism to urban mythology, but, no, it's legit. In fact, I'm merely one degree of separation from a story confirming its existence. Here goes... Recently divorced and back in the singles' scene, my friend, Tracy, was surprised at how tough it was to meet quality men. At lunch with her mom and aunt one day, she started sharing the challenges of dating after eight years off the market. But her Aunt Judy wasn't having it. "I don't know how you can even complain! What have you done to meet someone? Nothing! We have so many friends with nice, eligible sons, but you refuse to let us set you up. No wonder you're single! You're just not trying hard enough!"

True, in the vast majority of life's endeavors, increased effort equals increased probability of success. No need for dispute. But for every rule there's an exception, and, unfortunately, finding The One simply doesn't fit the *"effort = success"* equation. Because, trust me, there are a lot of women giving it all they've got, but they're still coming home empty-handed night after night.

Furthermore, what exactly constitutes trying hard *enough*? Who determines the level of acceptable effort? All the single women I know make regular and concerted overtures to meet men. We seek out occasions to interact with available bachelors all the time! We frequent hipster bars and coffeehouses, take our puppies to dog parks and our cats to hot, unattached veterinarians. We even buy groceries on "singles' night" at *Whole Foods*. What more do we have to do to convince our friends, family, coworkers, and whoever cares to weigh in on the issue that we're trying as hard as we possibly can?

Well, according to Tracy's Aunt Judy, you just need to let 'em set you up. Acquiesce. Give in. Put on your game face and accept that blind date with your grandmother's neighbor's brother's lawyer's step-son's best friend. You might as well concede. They'll badger you incessantly until you comply. You'll never win this battle, anyway. The opponent comes too well prepared! Armed with abundant folklore and old wives' tales, they weave elaborate yarns about women who met the loves of their lives on random fix-ups. And if you'd just try a little harder, it could happen for you, too!

Granted, set-ups have probably garnered a few happy matches over the last millennium, yet for every such instance, there are a million (or at least several thousand) disastrous scenarios. Mostly because when folks set us up, they simply don't think. Or, if they are thinking, they employ severely wacked reasoning. "Let's see, I have a single friend who is male. And I have another friend who is single and female. She's extroverted, outdoorsy, and a world traveler. He's introverted, prefers his computer to people, and at 35, has yet to leave his home state. Look at that! How fantastic! A match made in heaven! They'll live happily ever after for sure!"

I know they're only trying to help, but is it really so hard to see that most of the time we have *nothing* in common with the men they pick? As if the only criteria necessary for compatibility is complementary genitalia. *"He = man"; "she = woman"*. A perfect fit!

Then again, even if the guy *is* a halfway decent match for us, we may still shy away from the set-up, if we're smart. Why? Because letting a friend play Cupid is one of the most precarious dynamics you can introduce into your relationship. It's horribly risky! The pressure! The expectations! This seemingly innocent and supportive gesture can devastate your friendship.

Think about it. Essentially, a set-up presents a lose-lose situation for you and your matchmaking friend, unless, of course, you fall madly in love with Bachelor #1 the minute you lay eyes on him. If that happens, I'll take it all back because, clearly, that's a win-win (except that your girlfriend will feel entitled to be the maid of honor in your wedding, as a sort of finder's fee, and that might tick off your sister...) But anything short of love at first sight can lead to friendship fallout.

Let me explain. If, after the blind date, you decide you're not into him, be advised, your friend's going to take it personally. She'll say it's cool, of course, but that's a lie. In actuality, she'll be extremely upset and the closer her relationship with the guy, the more miffed she'll be. If it's her brother, watch out. It could completely ruin your friendship because by rejecting him, you're rejecting her. She may even lash out and tell you you're too picky! (See Chapter 3 for assistance.)

But what about the flip side? There's always the possibility you'll find the guy appealing, but he won't be feelin' you. That's no fun, either. Again, potential friendship fallout. Since in this case you're the one who's smitten, you'll be chomping at the bit to find out what he thought of you. You may even start stalking your friend, calling her ten times a day to see what sort of impression you made. Meanwhile, she's performing elite mental gymnastics to figure out a way to let you down gently. Now she feels bad about coming up with the whole idea and you're angry and humiliated. *Voilà!* A barrier in the midst of what used to be a perfectly decent friendship.

Clearly, if we're smart, we may steer clear of set-ups altogether—especially ones orchestrated by those close to us. After all, who wants to jeopardize a good friendship on the miniscule chance that the matchmaking might manufacture something special?

PSYCH 101: WHY THEY DO IT

They do it because they don't know what else to do. They say it because they don't know what else to say. Falling back on what they *do* know, the old equation of *"effort = success"*, they take a stab at it on our behalf in the form of a horribly hapless fix-up. Or maybe they're speaking from experience. Perhaps they were single once and tried really, really hard and let themselves get set up five times a week for five years and then finally met someone wonderful. Lucky them! Sometimes that happens. Sometimes it doesn't. But love isn't math, and there are no formulae and no algorithms. And actually, trying has very little to do with it.

Know that, even though it hurts when they say we're not trying, they don't mean to hurt us. Know that they're frustrated for us, not with us. Know that the insult of a ridiculously incompatible match is unintended. They just want to help. If they could change things, they would. And of course, they can't, so they say stupid things sometimes, like "you're not trying hard enough," and do stupid things other times, like fixing us up with guys we'd never be interested in. Hey, at least they didn't tell us to get back "out there"!

It just hasn't happened yet

As noted, blind dates and set-ups almost always involve painful emotional aftermath. Since these contrived meetings rarely work, more often than not, both parties leave disappointed and hurt. And *yes*, I mean both parties.

For example, let's say you've been set up with this guy, John. Both of you have been single for a while, so naturally, both of you approach the date with a bit of cynicism and low expectations. However, much to his surprise, John finds you to be attractive, intelligent, funny, and entertaining. And though you recognize that John, too, is attractive, intelligent, funny, and entertaining, you don't feel that "spark" or romantic connection. You therefore spend the entire date trying to remain polite and attentive, while not encouraging John. After dessert, you part ways and go home to lick your wounds.

John's injury is obvious. He feels rejected and disappointed. It hurts when romantic interest isn't reciprocated.

But you did the rejecting so you should leave unscathed, right? Wrong. Because though it was just one date, which you approached with much skepticism, still down deep a tiny, little part of you ignited a flicker of hope that he could be The One and things might actually work out for once. Sigh.

Yet far more deleterious shrapnel from the post-blind-date fallout entails the analyzing and second guessing yourself. *He was such a nice guy. I really wish I could've been attracted to him. He's got a great job, he's cute, and he cracked me up the whole time.*

What's my problem, anyway? Maybe I am too picky, like everyone says. Maybe I do think I'm too good for anybody. Maybe I'm a raging narcissist, basking in delusions of grandeur, destined to forever refuse every perfectly decent man who comes my way! You started the evening feeling single and lonely. You leave it feeling single and lonely *and* callous, mean, and unsure of yourself.

No one seems to understand any of this when they pressure us to pair up with every random recommendation we receive. See, I told you—both parties leave disappointed and hurt.

Ditto

Audrey Irvine, senior assignment manager for CNN, shared this snippet in a *Relationship Rant*, which she writes for CNN.com:

"Enter exhibit A: Female, 40 years old, single, career woman, no kids, victimized by 10 unsuccessful 'hookups' per year since the age of 35... I remember going to a barbecue where I didn't realize I was one of the entrées for another single man in attendance. Somewhere between eating potato salad and rocking out my best Beyoncé moves in the karaoke competition, it came to light that my friend thought this 'gentleman' and I were meant to meet.

As I wiped my sweaty brow and gazed at him in his circa-1970s outfit, I realized I had just auditioned for this guy. That's when I asked my friend what she possibly thought I had in common with this man outside of us both having a pulse. She had no answer except that we were both single. Shared interests, mutual attraction? Those got no consideration."[13]

Girl Talk

Dear Karin,

Absolutely. Definitely. I second the motion, etc. You're right about all this stuff, but you forgot the other annoying thing about matchmaking—when your friends talk up some guy and promise to introduce him to you and then never deliver!

This happens to me all the time! One of my friends will be like, "I've got the perfect guy for you," and then she'll go on and on about how fantastic he is and make me promise to meet him at a party or fundraiser or whatever. And at first I'll be a little dubious, but after an hour and a half of hearing how great he is, I'll get intrigued and want to see for myself.

But a week later I'm still waiting to hear the details on how I'm supposed to meet the guy. Do you think that party invitation ever arrives? No! Does the

Evite for the benefit show up in my inbox? Of course not! My girl goes back to her comfortable married life and forgets all about the fact that she made me fall madly in love with some guy I don't even know! Not nice!

And the best part is—these friends are the same ones who have the NERVE to tell me I'm not trying hard enough to meet men.

— *Janelle, 31*

Dear Janelle,

Dang. That's harsh. *You're* not trying hard enough, but *they* can't even make a phone call and arrange a double date? I feel your pain, girl. It's happened to me. It's happened to my single friends. We've all been there.

In fact, a few years ago my happily married brother persuaded my friend Kelly that she and his buddy *had* to meet each other. My brother spent an entire Sunday afternoon convincing her that they were destined to be together, Kelly and Andrew—a match made in heaven. And since she was single and pretty lonely at the time, she glommed onto the idea with a vengeance. She was like, "You know, it's crazy. I couldn't pick him out in a crowd, but I've got a hunch I'm gonna marry that Andrew Miller. I can feel it!" Sure, she was joking (kinda), but after all the hype, she wanted to at least meet him.

But do you think that rendezvous ever happened? You know it didn't. My brother's ADHD bounced him onto the next topic or person or whatever else was going on in his life and Kelly never heard another peep about her sure-to-be future husband.

You're right. It's not nice. But someone else has to write that book and tell the marrieds to follow through on their schemes. Some sort of "How to" book, maybe—*How to Not be a Jerk to Your Single Friends* or *How to Avoid Getting Your Girl's Hopes Up* or *Please Shut Up About That Great Guy If You're Just Going to Go Back to Your Happily Married Life and Never Actually Introduce Us to Him Anyway.* Okay, that last title wasn't the catchiest, but you get the idea.

— Karin

The Awful Truth

Remember, these scenes are not *based* on real stories. They *are* real stories!

DOUBLE BLIND

CAST.
ANDIE: single 28-year-old graduate student
ELAINE: random woman Andie does not know, but who goes to Andie's parents' church

BILL: single 30-year-old guy who, though very
nice, is nowhere near Andie's type

INTERIOR — CHURCH NARTHEX — DAY

Home from school for the weekend, Andie is
attending her parents' new church. After the
service, she waits for her mom and dad in the
narthex, a bit uncomfortable as she doesn't
know anyone.

> ELAINE
> Hi, Andie! It's sooooooo great to
> see you! How's school going?

> ANDIE
> Hi, um...

Andie searches her mind for a name, as she
can't remember if she's ever met this woman.

> ANDIE
> Well, school is going great,
> thanks...

> ELAINE
> Are you seeing anyone special?

> ANDIE
> Uh, no, I guess not really, I uh—

ELAINE
GREAT! Come with me. Quick!
I've got someone you need to meet!

Elaine grabs Andie's hand and drags her to the
other side of the narthex where Bill nervously
awaits.

ELAINE
[giddily] Andie, this is Bill.
Bill, this is Andie. I just <u>had</u> to
introduce you since you have
so much in common!
Wonderful! I'll leave you two
alone.

An awkward exchange of small talk ensues
after which Andie excuses herself as quickly as
possible and rushes for cover in the ladies'
room.

Lesson Learned: If you're single too long, people will
begin to take all kinds of liberties. If they determine
you aren't trying hard enough, they'll take matters into
their own hands—even if they have no clue who the
heck you are.

Guy Talk

Okay, so first of all, you ladies should know that guys get this same stuff—the pressure to meet our mom's best friend's gorgeous niece Lindsey who'll be in town for a weekend on her way back to grad school. And, oh my gosh, Guy and Lindsey just **HAVE** to meet each other. Then they break out their phones to show you no less than **70** pictures and start in with, "Isn't she stunning! Can you believe she's almost completed her Ph.D. in microbiology? She's only 29!" And I'm thinkin', *Sure, she's hot and all, but she lives halfway across the country and I failed high school bio. This ain't a match, people!*

But no, reason rarely prevails when dealing with middle-aged women and their matchmaking, so of course, the following weekend I find myself on a date with the beautiful and brilliant Lindsey. And yes, she's everything they said she'd be—and I'm smitten.

But here's the kicker—I can tell they had to twist her arm even harder than mine to make this date happen. She's *so* obviously not interested in me or what I'm about and she clearly has way better things to do than hang out at a sports bar with a biology flunky. And somehow, despite my sincere efforts, she remains unimpressed as I try to regale her with one of my all-time best high school stories—the time when I stuck my dissected frog in my ex-girlfriend's locker. It was awesome! She screamed bloody murder and passed out cold in the middle of the hallway... (Wow! You're kidding! This story *didn't* impress the lovely Lindsey? — Karin) **Hey, I was trying to connect on the biology thing!** (Right. Good plan. — Karin)

Whatever. So what I'm getting at is—Karin's right. Don't agree to any fix-ups just to appease people. If you're in the mood, go ahead and give it a shot. But if not, take the high road, do the right thing, and give a guy a break. Don't go out on the date in the first place. 'Cause really—and I know I have to keep reminding you—guys have feelings, too.

— Guy

See, this is why we need to hear from the fellas. I couldn't have said it better myself.

— Karin

Selfie

Oh how I tried. I really, really tried.

I tried by agreeing to a slew of blind dates and

set ups. I tried by getting back out there. I tried by forcing myself to make relationships work regardless of nagging doubts and even complete disinterest.

Once, while at a church singles' event, I met Jamie who I convinced myself to go out with—despite having no physical attraction to him—because I'd bought into the "you're too picky" accusations and figured I should try harder to give him a chance. When the chemistry failed to develop, I eventually broke it off and, though I did the rejecting, I still felt the sting of the tanked relationship. I doubted myself, felt like a jerk for unintentionally leading him on, and wondered, for the millionth time, if maybe I *was* being too picky.

After a mediocre/not-horrible date with Ryan, I kept going out with him because he was cute enough, looked good on paper, and despite my misgivings, I feared I couldn't trust my instincts anymore. I'd persuaded myself that, as an adult, I couldn't expect to feel the fireworks and butterflies of puppy love. After eight months, things fizzled out and looking back, I have the impression that Ryan, too, had tried to manufacture feelings for me that he really didn't have. I guess guys get told they're too picky, too!

So, on my 30th birthday, when that nice guy approached me, I tried to give him a chance. I tried to fall for him during the four years we dated. I tried to ignore the voice in my head telling me it didn't feel right. I tried to feel excited when he proposed. I tried to play the role of blushing, gushing bride even though the thought of a life with him petrified me. I tried to carry on with him for reasons that seemed compelling—my parents worried about me, most of my friends were married, and the tick-tock of my biological clock reverberated in my ears. I tried to convince myself that whatever I thought was missing from the relationship must be either inconsequential or evidence of some sort of pathology on my part. I tried to love him because he was a good guy and deserved a devoted wife.

I tried. I tried. I tried.

Shout Out!

So to my smart, sexy, savvy singletons I say this: No matter how much people try to tell you otherwise, it's not a matter of effort. *"E = MC²"* doesn't translate to *"Effort = Man Catching²"*. If only finding a guy were as easy as comprehending mass-energy equivalence! Anytime a fix up feels too forced, allow yourself to take a pass. No pressure, no problem... because single is the new black!

Part 2

a few things you may be doing to complicate matters

chapter 7

Don't Compare Yourself to Your Married Friends!

keeping up with the Joans

My friends used to tell me stuff like this when we were younger and they were married. And I kept thinking something was wrong because I didn't have someone in my life. Then I met my guy and I've been with him for 5 years (I was picky, by the way—we should be). But what's interesting is my friends are now either divorced or really dissatisfied with their marriages. All that time I felt I was missing out on being in love and being married and now they're not happy and they want to be single again!

— Mandy, 42

Comparison games. They're not just played by suburban couples trying to "keep up with the Joneses". We women compete in a Powder Puff League of this sport—"Keeping Up with the *Joans*". And the longer you stay single, the lower you rank, since you have yet to score the only point that matters in this match—marriage.

But your friends have much better luck. One by one they hit grand slams, skip around the bases, and march toward the home-plate altar, which, interestingly, alters the delicate dynamics of your relationships. That lovely day in June granted her more than a new name and a bit of left-hand bling. It also garnered her a measure of social credibility and respect reserved solely for women bearing the title of "Mrs.". Friends who were once on your level advance and become your superiors. The balance tips and it's disconcerting. Some women lord it over you, *à la* "Things are so different for me now—you'll understand once you're married." Most don't. But nevertheless, you feel it. In society's eyes, and maybe in each other's eyes, you're no longer the same.

You wonder how it all happened, anyway. *What did Joan do to land a CEO while I'm still meeting bozos! Seriously? I dated way more guys than she did in college! Besides, she's not as pretty as I am! And she's such a complainer. Plus, she's got ugly feet. Has Mark seen her in sandals?*

Annoyed by your own pettiness, you check yourself. *What's my problem? What's with all this jealousy? Besides, I'm totally happy for her! I don't begrudge her a bit. After all, she's one of my best friends.*

Still, you marvel at how love's been so easy for her yet so tough for you. In an attempt to discern the secret of her success, you take stock of what she has to offer versus what you bring to the table. And that's all it takes. Just like that, without even realizing it, you've started a round of "Keeping Up with the Joans".

See how easy it is to slip into that way of thinking? You're not catty! You're not envious of your friends! You can't believe you got sucked into playing silly comparison games in the first place. But you did. And absolutely no good will come of it.

Because a round of "Keeping Up with the Joans" proves infuriating for two reasons. First of all, you're irritated with yourself for stooping to make parallels because it's trifling and lame and you know it.

But perhaps even more maddening is you can't really pinpoint where you fall short. In fact, you think you measure up pretty well to your friend, yet your girl's the one who nabbed a man. Hmmm. How'd that happen?

Let me take a stab at it—and I'm not trying to be harsh, I'm really not, but this book is meant to encourage single women, so I'm worried about *your* feelings, not the feelings of your happily married friends. I'm just going to be frank here for a minute.

It's not that I want to put anyone down, but the point is, and you know this if you're honest with yourself, some of your married friends settled. They may never admit it, but they did. So you *can't* compare yourselves to them because you're holding out for true love. And as for their husbands? They're not your type! So why would you be jealous? Because you got caught up in comparisons, that's why!

Plus, when playing "Keeping Up with the Joans", you inadvertently subscribe to the bogus logic that since you're still single, you're losing the competition and are therefore off your game. Right. As if that makes any sense! So the average 35-year-old married woman is superior to the average 35-year-old single woman? The wife has fewer emotional hang-ups than her single counterpart just because she's married? Or she's more talented and has a better personality? Seriously? Where's the sense in that? What about the wives that settled? Shouldn't we be concerned about *their* issues?

But no one sees it that way. It's as if once a woman marries, she's *arrived* and even if she has to spend the rest of her life with a complete tool, it doesn't matter, because at least she's *married*. And we all buy into it. When actually, you took the harder path and didn't settle for a dork like some of your friends did! (Okay, that was a little harsh—sorry!)

The tragedy lies in the fact that we minimize, or completely ignore, the courageous decision we've made to wait for the right person. Instead of seeing ourselves as gutsy and self-sufficient in our singleness, we suspect we possess myriad weaknesses. Come on! It's exactly the opposite! We singles risk being alone forever, refusing to resign ourselves to a mediocre relationship. That's pretty brave and impressive!

We enjoy our *own* company on weekend nights. We manage our *own* bank accounts and select our *own* retirement plans. We cheer on our *own* careers and dry our *own* tears. But instead of giving ourselves our *own* "high fives", we search for imperfections and scramble to bookstores to identify the *Ten Stupid Things You Do to Chase Away Mr. Right* or *Mistakes Women Make After 30 That Keep Them from Walking Down the Aisle*. We downplay the chancy, courageous choice we've made while elevating the easy, wussy choice made by some of our friends. Do you see what we do to ourselves?

Granted, not all your friends settled. And a few of them have great husbands—smart, funny, accomplished guys—the type you'd like to end up with. Well, I've got a newsflash for you. I *know* the secret to their success and I'm here to reveal this highly sensitive, classified information. Are you ready? Brace yourself. *THEY GOT LUCKY!* Yep, you heard me. It was just plain luck. They happened to meet an amazing guy in freshman English and were able to avoid all the angst and uncertainty of independent, single adulthood. Pure luck.

But that's not how we perceive it. We compare ourselves to our friends, strike up a round of "Keeping Up with the Joans", and assume the wives did something right while we keep messing up.

PSYCH 101: WHY WE DO IT

Why do we judge ourselves against our friends? Why insist we're flawed? Why minimize our gutsy choice?

Let's start with society and I know I keep pointing the finger at this nebulous "society" thing, but, truly, society is guilty in this case with its simple formula of *"Married = Good / Single = Bad"*. Our culture conceptualizes singles as overgrown children trapped in adult bodies, selfishly wasting away our days in irresponsible laziness and frivolity. Meanwhile, married people contribute responsibly and generously to all factions of civilization in an industrious, committed, and mature manner.

I wish I'd made up such impressions for effect, but unfortunately, research backs these assessments. Since we're taking Psych 101 here and not a grad course I'll leave out the details, but studies find most people, married and unmarried alike, view singles in a much more negative light than those who are married. Meaning, even we singles look down on ourselves and each other.[14]

This mentality sneaks into countless elements of our daily existence and sometimes, no matter how strong we are, we get exhausted. Weary of fending off the *"Single = Bad"* formula, we give in. *If I compare myself to Joan maybe I can figure it all out—what she's got that I don't, what she's doing right that I'm doing wrong. I'm tired of being inferior. For once, I want to win this game.*

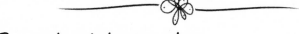

It just hasn't happened yet

Okay, I admit it. In supporting my single girls, I played some comparison games myself. I pitted you against your married friends, suggesting they sold out and you didn't. I compared their wimpy choice to your courageous one. I insinuated they didn't have the guts to go it alone, so they caved and coupled.

Am I sorry? Nope. Again, I wasn't trying to rip on your married friends. That's not the point. But single women take hits all the time. People offend you at every turn with their insensitive appraisals and irrational perspectives. Prevailing societal conceptions accuse you of insufficiency and ineptitude. You unwittingly internalize such judgments and then do battle with the voices in your head saying you're disturbed, damaged, and doomed.

So, this chapter brought you a different message: one about how cool, gutsy, and fabulous you actually are!

Ditto

Maybe we wouldn't try so hard to keep up with the Joans if singles were accorded the same respect as other adults—if the assessment of our worth reflected our contribution to society, as opposed to our marital status.

And just to set the record straight here and now, the research of Dr. Bella DePaulo finds that single adults are typically *more* generous with charitable contributions and acts of service to the community than married adults.[15]

Nevertheless, pejorative perceptions remain, as noted by Miriam Greenwald of UnmarriedAmerica.org:

"Not all married people are mature or wise... Why is even the most dysfunctional couple elevated above the best adjusted single person? Because according to society the very fact of being perpetually single brings into question everything else. Or if you are truly alone, how, according to others, can you by definition be well adjusted? Since only the credentials of marriage attest to 'normal' adjustment!"[16]

Girl Talk

Dear Karin,

You nailed me in this chapter. You basically told my exact story. Not to sound like I'm bragging, but in college, I was "it"! I was president of my sorority, fraternity sweetheart four years in a row, and as for guys? Please, I think I spent maybe two weekends alone during my entire college career. I mean, it was so easy then. I'd break up with one boyfriend and meet another in the caf the very next day! Done and done! And again, I'm not trying to blow my own horn, but really, I went out with way more guys than any of my friends.

But check this out. My roommate, Alyssa, well, she didn't go out with anyone from freshman to junior year. Maybe a date here and there, but nothing serious at all. I don't think she went to even one Homecoming. Then all of a sudden she meets this guy, Rob, in a senior seminar and BAM! It's over. They dated for three years, moved to Portland together, and now they're about to buy a condo in the Pearl district. Oh, and did I mention the ROCK on her left hand? Yeah, it's gotta be three carats.

And I love Alyssa and all, but how did she hit the jackpot and I'm still going out with crack pots?
— Holly, 27

Dear Holly,

Your story just proves my point. All those years in college, you're out with a different guy every night while Alyssa's back in the dorm room knitting socks and baking cookies. You know she's a great girl, but she's not turning too many heads. Until that one day it happens—connection! She meets him and, as you put it, it's over. Of course, you know Alyssa's not prettier or smarter or funnier than you. And she's certainly no more emotionally stable or less neurotic than you just because she happened to run into Rob in senior seminar. She's not a better "catch" than you. She just met her match and you haven't yet. Simple as that.

Oh, and you didn't mention it, which was gracious of you, but I'm betting that, although from time to time you feel jealous of their relationship, you probably wouldn't want to marry a guy like Rob anyway. Am I right? 'Cause really, if you could have been happy with a "Rob" type, you probably would have met an equivalent version of him in *your* senior seminar. Don't you think?

— Karin

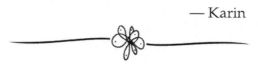

The Awful Truth

Remember, these scenes are not *based* on real stories. They *are* real stories!

MAID OF DISHONOR

CAST.
TORIE: 28-year-old maid of honor. Single.
NATALIA: 28-year-old bride.

INTERIOR — HOTEL BANQUET HALL — NIGHT

The Garcia/Petersen wedding reception is in full swing. The best man has just delivered his toast and now passes the microphone to Torie, the maid-of-honor. Swaying a bit as she stands, it's clear she's already had several cocktails.

>   TORIE
>   Hi there. I'm Torie... Um... So
>   I'm really excited to have the
>   chance to toast the lovely Natalia
>   and her handsome groom, Tyler.

TORIE pauses to allow for applause

>   TORIE
>   You know, it's a beautiful thing
>   when someone finds true love.

And as Natalia's best friend since—I don't even know how long— [to Natalia] How old were we when we met, Nat?

NATALIA
[smiling] Like 4 or 5!

We hear an "Awww" from the guests.

TORIE
Exactly! It was Mrs. Holland's kindergarten class! Yeah, so we've been like sisters from the beginning and of course, over the years I've cried with her when she's gone through heartache after heartache after heartache after heartache...

The crowd laughs.

TORIE
The funny thing is, here she is getting married and I'm still single, but growing up, I always had a boyfriend and Natalia hardly ever did. Let's see, in 7th grade Barry Cohen dumped her right before the sock hop, and

Jamie Hannigan stood her up for junior prom, and Troy Davis refused her invitation to Sadie Hawkins—which was cold because they were *really* close friends if you know what I mean...

Guests cough and shift uncomfortably in their seats.

TORIE
Right, yeah—that wasn't pretty, trust me!

TORIE pauses and chugs the rest of her champagne.

TORIE
And then we got out of college, moved to the city and things really got dicey. I mean, I think we can all agree we thought this day might never come—what with Natalia's propensity for one night stands, and all...

As TORIE pauses for laughter (which doesn't come), the groom stands up with his best man and escorts TORIE out of the reception hall.

Lesson Learned: The jealousy that consumes us when we indulge in comparison games is super-unattractive and hardly the way friends, let alone members of a bridal party, should act toward one another. Besides, ladies, we're just way too fabulous for that!

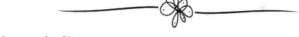

Guy Talk

Okay, I'm sorry, but this chapter was kinda hilarious for me! Aren't aggression and competitiveness supposed to be linked to testosterone? What's wrong with you women? All the catfighting and carrying on!

Maybe I just don't get it because guys don't think this way. Certainly not when it comes to being married, anyway—we usually get dragged down the aisle kicking and screaming, right? So we don't see our friends as superior to us just because we haven't found ourselves a wife.

Maybe we lack the jealousy gene or something because we definitely don't go for the jugular the way women do. It's like, if my buddy shows up to a party with some gorgeous woman I think, "What's up with that? If that joker can do it so can I! I gotta get me a hottie, too." But I don't seethe about it and hold it against him and get mad because I dated more cheerleaders than he did in high school.

No offense, Karin. But this is really a nasty window into chick culture.

— Guy

Wait a minute, so you're trying to tell me guys don't get jealous of each other? Are you kidding? With all the posturing and chest thumping and cruising around in hot rods with silicone-enhanced candy on each arm? Come on, Guy.

I think I see your point, though. But it all goes back to how we're evaluated. A woman's worth is determined by her relationships, while a man's net worth determines his value. So with men, we might see a little more cut-throat activity in the business realm, whereas with women, the backstabbing occurs in the social milieu. Come to think of it, have you ever been to a trading floor?

I rest my case.

— Karin

Selfie

I admit it. For a while I played *Keeping Up with the Joans*. But I got pretty tired of losing.

The first several years post-college proved toughest for me in this realm. Later, in my thirties, I'd settled into my path, embracing the independence and strength I'd gained by virtue of flying solo through early adulthood. But initially, it was hard watching my friends step into the conventional path of marriage and children, leaving me behind to fend for myself. I wanted a life like theirs, and sometimes I felt left out and isolated.

With age, I've realized most women feel alienated from their peers at one time or another—maybe we struggle to get pregnant when everyone else seems to conceive easily or we draw up divorce papers while girlfriends celebrate 10th anniversaries or we meander around in dead-end jobs as colleagues leap up the ladder two rungs at a time. I know this now—the ubiquity of perceived alienation. But in my twenties, I felt alone—like I was the only one who couldn't get it together. To me, it seemed my life continued to careen off course while my friends' lives stabilized and became secure. We used to have everything in common—not so much anymore.

As my girls and I moved in different directions, misunderstandings abounded. How could they not? We now lacked the common ground we'd shared in our dorm room days. I remember one time, maybe five or six years after we'd graduated, one of my college roommates, Britt, and I were on the phone and she recounted a recent exchange she'd had with a mutual friend who'd been talking about how she couldn't believe I wasn't married and how lonely I must be. Britt snapped back with, "What? Karin is fine! Don't you worry about her! She's having the time of her life in Chicago!" While I thanked Britt for shielding me from misplaced pity, internally I thought, *Yeah, but that's not completely true. Sometimes I do feel isolated and worry I'll be alone forever.*

But there was no way I'd risk tarnishing Britt's image of me. I liked her bold, "I don't need anybody" version of Karin better than the not-always-feeling-strong, "I really miss having a boyfriend" Karin—who was, admittedly, the more accurate description of my twenty-something self.

Shout Out!

So to my smart, sexy, savvy, single friends I say this: No matter how much you compare yourselves to your married friends, you'll never figure out what they did "right" and you did "wrong". They aren't any better or worse than you or any more or less messed up. Please—no more "Keeping Up with the Joans". You, kitten, are way too cool to play that catty game. Besides, some of your friends wore white before it was right and that's so last season... single is the new black.

chapter 8

It's Okay to Take a Break from Online Dating!

it's just a singles' bar in cyberspace

It's like I feel this pressure to be online all the time. Like the man of my dreams could be a mouse click away and what if I miss him because I let my FindTheOne.com subscription expire?

— Carla, 37

And yes, I know your friend, Chrissy, met the love of her life online. So did my BFF, Vanessa, and guess what? Even though she met her husband and the father of her two beautiful kids on the Internet she *still* talks about how much she hated every minute of the online scene.

It's not that dating sites never work. Obviously, they occasionally do the trick. With the enormous number of people putting up profiles nowadays, eventually some get lucky. Which, of course, proves annoying for everyone else because their success provides platitudinal ammo for those on the outside— *i.e.,* another way for people to claim you're doing something wrong which is why you're single: "But you haven't even given eHusband.com a chance! You said yourself that Chrissy met her fiancé on that site!"

So after getting reamed enough, you figure you better at least try it. It can't hurt anything and it's got to increase your odds of finding a boyfriend, right? Well, not necessarily.

Think about it. If you walked into a coworker's cocktail party on any given Saturday night, no matter how many guys showed up, you'd likely find yourself attracted to only a certain portion of them. Let's say roughly 20% of the fellas would pique your interest, with the other 80% leaving you completely flat. Naturally, of the ones you deemed appealing, half would drive you nuts the minute they opened their mouth—unless, of course, these guys bore a resemblance to Jude Law, in which case you'd put up with innumerable asinine utterances just to bask in their physical perfection for a while. But barring that potentiality, you're left with a possible connection with roughly one out of every ten guys. Put those percentages to work on LoveOfALifetime.com and you'll see what you're dealing with. Loads of men. No increase, however, in the proportion of those with prospective compatibility.

But since there are more men online than at your coworker's cocktail party, if we're talking sheer numbers, we definitely increase our chances of success by trying the websites, right? Not necessarily, and here's why. If the population of gentlemen cruising around online is representative of the population of gentlemen at your coworker's cocktail party, then, yes, you'll have a probable connection with roughly 10% of them. But if the online population doesn't mirror the demographic of your coworker's party, then, sadly, that percentage will probably be less. In fact, one might argue that devoting too much time to finding a boyfriend online potentially *decreases* your odds of finding a partner.

Why? Because the online thing is a complete free-for-all! At least when you run into a prospect while going about your business, you have a reasonable chance of having one or two things in common. The very fact that you happened upon each other while living your typical day in your typical world suggests some promise. If you bump into a cute guy at your favorite restaurant, you apparently have similar tastes in cuisine. Or if you strike up a conversation with a fellow attendee at a professional conference, you clearly work in similar industries. Or if your introduction occurs at a dinner party, you share mutual friends and travel in similar circles. But if you meet someone online, it's possible that the only thing you have in common is your ability to enter a URL address—which might not get you very far once the relationship begins.

Another reason your odds have *not* increased involves the anonymity of cyberspace. Okay, how can I put this delicately? Let's go back to the men from your coworker's cocktail party. Remember the 80% you found unattractive? Well, in a real-life situation, although some of those fellows might be interested in you, most of them would readily pick up your vibe of disinterest and leave you alone. Admittedly, a few clueless characters would cruise over armed with a drink and a bad pickup line, but the majority would recognize they didn't have a chance, at least not until they'd garnered some liquid courage.

Not so in cyberworld. Again, I'm trying to be sensitive here, but if you post a profile online, you're going to get hits from guys who would *never ever* have the nerve to approach you in a bar or dance club. Not in a million years! But that cyberdistance gives all kinds of men all kinds of guts.

PSYCH 101: WHY WE DO IT

We do it for any number of reasons. Perhaps friends have badgered us into trying harder (see Chapter 6) but instead of rustling up a blind date, they hopped online and put together a profile for us on Mismatch.com, and we indulge them in order to get them off our backs. Or maybe this week's water cooler gossip consisted of a slew of online dating fairy tales and you got caught up in the hype. Of course, the television commercials could have caught your eye; they can be pretty persuasive on a solitary Saturday night. Or then again, you could have just been really bored.

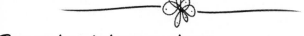

It just hasn't happened yet

Which, by the way, is what you'll need to be—really bored—because online dating takes up a *lot* of time! First off, you'll spend hours trying to write the perfect biographical sketch, certain your entire future rests in your profile's packaging so it better be good! You'll want to come across as cute, but not cutesy. Funny, but not wacky. Intelligent, but not nerdy. Composing the document will take a minimum of six or seven hours, after which you'll force all your girlfriends to preview it and give you feedback before you go live. An utter waste of time, by the way, since no man in the history of online dating has read even a single word of a woman's profile. Please, they go straight for the pictures.

Which leads to the next time-consuming operation: selecting your photos—more painful and arduous decisions! You want to look beautiful, but not stuck up. Professional, but not stiff. Sexy, but not slutty. Though horribly laborious, at least the hours consumed by this activity pay off since your pictures will be carefully and repeatedly scrutinized by several thousand men in cyberland—a somewhat disconcerting concept in and of itself, if you stop to think about it.

And finally, after completing your profile, you'll take a turn perusing what the gentlemen have to offer. Contrary to the fantastical contemplations of your married friends, this exercise bears absolutely no resemblance to kids frolicking in candy stores. In fact, the whole tortuous ordeal typically drains and discourages you further as you click through umpteen million profiles of dudes saying the exact same thing:

- I'm a [*middle management position*] at [*your town's big firm or business*].

- I love going to [*random indie band you've never heard of*] shows.

- I'm the HUGEST [*your city's major league baseball team*] fan ever!

- I love moonlit walks on the beach [*Liar!*].

Mind you, all of the above give you no useful information whatsoever because it describes *every single man* between the ages of 21 and 71. They might as well have written that they breathe on a regular basis and rely on food to nourish their bodies. Furthermore, as evidenced by the bit about loving moonlit walks on the beach, cyberdistance encourages truth stretching in myriad ways...

So you scroll and scroll and troll and troll and as your eyes glaze over you feel increasingly bored and hopeless. But the worst part? On top of the apathy and *ennui*, you also feel mean, cruel, and harsh. Why? Because pulling up a profile awakens your inner critic—*Oh, I don't think so! Please! He calls that an athletic build?* And *Are you kidding me? There is no way this dude is 32!* Or *This guy is so not cute to me! And neither is he... and neither is he... and neither is he...* More often than not, you end up more disheartened than before you got online. You start wondering if the two hours per night you devote to perusing profiles would be much better spent snuggled up in bed with a cat and a good book.

Earlier in the chapter I said it couldn't hurt anything to do a little online dating. Yeah, well I take it all back.

Ditto

In her article, "Why I Hate Online Dating" writer Nicole Rupersburg argues that finding love on a website closely resembles, well, shopping for a car.

"Sure, you might have a whole list of specifications and options you would *like* to have, but you also understand that finding that perfect ONE is probably all but impossible, so you're already going into it with the idea that you'll probably have to settle. But you accept the reality of this and begin your diligent search, looking at an endless stream of pictures and scouring details, making comparisons—this one is a newer model, but *this* one has a clean title and less mileage—in the hopes that you'll eventually find something 'good enough'. Because you know, at some point, you have stop searching and just pick something already.

And that's what online dating is for—finding that 'good enough' guy or girl after sifting through an endless sea of selfies and self-advertisements before landing on one that satisfies most, though not all, of your checklist items. You 'favorite' each other the way you add items to your Amazon Wish List or Pin recipes you want to try later, then you schedule an in-person interview during which you'll have all manners of nonversation, while in your head furiously trying to calculate whether or not this person should advance to the next round.

It is strategic and calculated and the absolute antithesis of romantic.

And this is why I hate online dating: Not because of the 'stigma' and not because it isn't practical, but because it feels so much like love brokering."[17]

Girl Talk

Dear Karin,

I am so over online dating. I'm sick of it! I hate it! It just makes me feel like crap!

Here's why: I had a date last Sunday with a guy I met online. He was okay looking, but soooooooooo boring. All he talked about for two hours was fantasy football and golf! Do I look like I care about either one of those things? But of course, I'm nice as pie during dinner, laughing, smiling "Wow, that's fascinating! Blah, blah, blah... lie, lie, lie." So then we're wrapping things up and getting ready to leave and he goes, "Have a nice Thanksgiving. Good luck." And I think, "Are you kidding me? You're not going to call me?!? You're dissing me after I put up with your monologue on driving irons and dynasty leagues?!? Well, screw you, Mr. I-am-so-boring-I-make-my-dates-want-to-poke-their-eyes-out-with-a-fork!"

I'm so sick and tired of being rejected. I know I shouldn't feel this way, but I do. And everyone's like, "Just go online!" Well, actually I hate to break it to them, but going online does absolutely nothing but make me feel bad. Either I have horrible dates like this one or the guys I'm actually interested in email me for weeks but never call! At this point, even if I'm not all that interested, it would be nice for SOMEONE to call. No, I should take that back. I did have one guy call, but unfortunately, he was utterly nuts!

I feel like I'm in such a bad place with all this, but how else am I supposed to feel? I can't even find Mr. Meantime, never mind Mr. Right!

Sorry to rant and rave, I'm just a little frustrated. I quit GetMarried.com and I'm for sure done with ConnectWithSomeone.com. I've decided to chuck it all and keep focusing on myself.

I'm so defeated by this online business, I got nothin' left.

— Whitney, 35

Dear Whitney,

Thanks for your candor. I'm sure it wasn't easy given how cruddy you're feeling right now. I know for a fact the single women reading your letter are fully empathizing with you; we've all been there at one point or another.

One thing you mentioned really stood out to me—how everyone tells you, "Just go online!" It's another one of the infuriating comments people are forever throwing our way. Clearly, most of them have never had to pursue the awkwardness of Internet dating because if they had, they'd realize there's no "just" about it. It's a highly laborious and involved activity, not to mention possibly expensive.

And your rotten experience gives a perfect example of how risky and painful online dating can be. You get punched in the gut and feel completely rejected by guys you didn't even find attractive in the first place! Still, that rejection stings... Great.

You've been feeling lonely for a while, and now you get to feel lonely *and* rejected. Wow! What a great experience this "just go online" thing turned out to be! Thanks for the fantastic advice, everybody!

— Karin

The Awful Truth

Remember, these scenes are not *based* on real stories. They *are* real stories!

NOTMEETINGANYONE.COM

CAST.
ANNETTE: 36-year-old single, HR manager

RITA: Dating website Customer Service Representative

INTERIOR — ANNETTE'S APARTMENT — DAY

Annette is on the phone with Rita, a customer service representative of a popular dating website.

                    RITA
Thank you for calling MeetSomeone Customer Care. This is Rita.

                  ANNETTE
Hi, Rita. I've got a few concerns with my MeetSomeone.com membership. I've been with the program for two months now and, frankly, I find this service to be very unsuccessful in finding me a match. I've communicated with several men up until the emailing process and then they fail to follow through. I've nudged them, as stated in your website's recommendations, but still nothing. Could you please explain how I go about getting a refund?

RITA

Annette, we appreciate your concern and we're here to offer assistance. First, I'd like to highly recommend you consider retaking the Relationship Questionnaire. We have six psychologists constantly researching and updating the Questionnaire and we're confident that upon retaking it, your ability to be matched will be that much greater.

ANNETTE

No, thank you, Rita. I'm not interested in retaking the questionnaire. I put a significant amount of time and thought into the questions the first time. I highly doubt my core opinions and values have changed dramatically in the past two months.

RITA

That's understandable, Annette. May I make another suggestion? As you have already nudged your matches, I recommend you close communication with those who have not yet responded to your efforts by providing the reason "This match never responded to my request to communicate."

ANNETTE

Thanks for the tip, Rita, but I always close the matches after I nudge them and they don't respond. By the way, the "nudge" option, in my opinion, is not helpful. I have not yet had anyone respond to the "nudge". It's humiliating to have to nudge anyway, which basically translates to "I'm desperate and need your attention." Maybe the men just don't have the energy to hit the "close" button. If that's the case, I'd rather not date someone that lazy anyway.

RITA

Okay. Well then, that's not the problem. May I share another suggestion that may prove successful? Posting photos is a great way to engage your matches and get conversations flowing. I see you already have six great pictures, and I would encourage you to consider adding as many as possible. This can truly help your match understand the many aspects of your personality and lifestyle, those qualities that make you who you are.

ANNETTE

Honestly, Rita, I feel six photos is quite appropriate. My pictures are current and show me in a variety of settings. Is this a dog-and-pony show or a dating site? Not to mention the fact that most of the men's pictures look more like mug shots from jail! Some of the guys actually take selfies in their bathroom mirrors. Personally, I'd prefer not to date someone who uses a camera in the bathroom. And a lot of the men post no pictures at all. But I'm supposed to put up 27?

RITA

Annette, I hear your concerns and I'm sorry you've not been successful so far. I'd like to ask you to reconsider taking to heart some of the suggestions I mentioned.

ANNETTE

So basically you're telling me that somehow it's my fault these men aren't interested in me or that my profile is not eye-catching enough. Thanks a lot. You know, it seems like the pervasive view of single women is "What are they doing wrong? Why can't they get a man?" Does anyone consider how much time and effort we invest in finding a partner? Blaming a single woman assumes there's something wrong with her. That's a pretty sad viewpoint—especially for a dating website. Actually Rita, I'm tired of talking about this and clearly you're reading off some sort of script so we're not getting anywhere at all. May I please just have my refund?

RITA

Again, Annette, I'd like to reiterate that I hear your concerns but I regret that we cannot process your request for a refund. Please be aware that early termination of your account does not result in a prorated refund. After the trial period has expired, we require that you stay the entire length of your subscription.

ANNETTE
Rita, your policy is ridiculous! This is a "service" you provide and if the service is not given, a refund should be issued!

Rita pauses.

RITA
Thank you for calling, Annette. The good news is, we have 15,000 new users registering every day. We're confident we'll help you find the love of your life.

Lesson learned: Online dating is a business. We forget that because the industry involves our love lives, but it's still a for-profit venture, ladies. Simply put, they want your money. The next time someone tells you to "just go online" let them read this little exchange. Maybe they'll get the picture.

Guy Talk

Let me take a minute to defend my half of the species because I'm not sure what's up with some of Karin's rhetoric here. For one, not all men lie on their online profiles (as Karin insinuated) and some guys don't like baseball (although I don't personally know any) and some of us truly do like walks on the beach (especially if there's the chance of a moonlight skinny dip). C'mon, Karin! What's with all the sexist statements?

I do have to agree with her, though, that the online thing can be a shot in the dark. But it's like that for guys, too. Women misrepresent themselves in their profiles just as often as men do. Sometimes your date shows up and you know for a fact her profile picture was taken a minimum of 10 years and 40 pounds ago. Or one time, I went out with a woman who, after a drink or two, made it quite clear she was in the market for a corporate type making high six figures. I was thinking, "Did this gold-digger somehow miss that I'm a writer and I checked the under $50,000 income box?"

So I get why you're frustrated at times, but then again, it doesn't hurt to try, right?   (I take it you didn't actually read the whole chapter then, Guy. I made it clear that sometimes it *does* hurt to try! — Karin)

Oh yeah, my bad. I forgot how painful it is for you women. When you're ripping these guys' profiles to shreds and lamenting that none of them are good enough for you, it makes you feel like a big, fat meany (actually, I've got another word for it, but...) Yeah, that's rough, ladies, because who wants to feel judgmental and harsh when you're really being, well— judgmental and harsh! "Woe is me! I'm too perfect for any of these mooks, and it's so hurtful to realize it!" Nice.

All I'm saying is give us a break every once in a while! Go out with the dude whose picture is a little goofy because he's not the most photogenic person alive or hold back on writing a guy off just because he has yet to acquire vacation property. A lot of these fellas are shy and nervous and it's gonna show up on their profile. Give 'em a chance to show up in person and make a case for themselves.

— Guy

Well then. I'm not going to even dignify certain elements of the preceding statement by attempting to defend my position. I'll simply reiterate that online dating *is* risky and *can* hurt both parties involved.

Guys ridicule our profiles, too, and we get rejected, as well (see Whitney's letter). But, as I always say, I asked for a guy's opinion so... Be careful what you ask for; you just might get it.

— Karin

Selfie

How I resisted the online scene! I did *not* want to go there! Posting pictures and providing personal information for all to see—no thanks! I had no interest whatsoever! But after a particularly long dry spell, I, like most of us on the prowl, caved and let my friend construct a profile for me.

Now truth be told, it's possible I enjoyed perhaps 2 to 3 minutes of my time online. But for the most part, I found the experience pretty darn unbearable. Don't get me wrong—I know online dating works for many, many people. It just wasn't my scene. I resented the hours it took to scroll through hundreds of profiles and I detested the requisite emailing overkill before a first date materialized. Who's got time for that?

I actually met one really nice guy who I saw for several months, but most of the men cruising the online scene seemed rather flaky. After three weeks of sporadic emailing, we'd finally get together and have a couple decent dates. Then they'd go missing for a period of time, often resurfacing later with a renewed urgency to pursue me.

I didn't put it all together at the time but a theme emerged as I interviewed women for this book. Many reported a belief that the online format provides men with way too many options, *i.e.* your date might think you're smart, sweet, and sexy but once he gets home he'll be tempted to hop back into cyberspace to see if he can find someone who's just a little smarter, sweeter, and sexier. So we're constantly competing with the prospect of a better version of us just a mouse click away.

Maybe that's what happened when the guys went M.I.A. Maybe not. I don't really care. I just know I found the whole experience awkward and arduous.

Shout Out!

So to my smart, sexy, savvy, singletons I say this: Going online won't guarantee you'll meet the love of your life. If it's fun for you, go for it! But internet dating isn't the only game in town so if it's played out for you, take your ball and go home. Kick off your cleats and slip on a dress—you know which color—because single is the new black.

chapter 9

Don't Get Back Together with Your Ex-Boyfriend!

the definition of insanity. . .

Tonight was a gem. First, I made plans to have dinner with an ex. Smart. Then, I was feeling girlie and frisky and decided to text a different ex, to ask him if he wanted to make out. Seriously, who does that? Apparently I do. His response was that he didn't think it would be a good idea and that we should probably discuss it later. I told him there's nothing to discuss, I'm just looking for fun. Just making out, no strings attached. There's a reason why we didn't work out, no need to rehash that. Now we have plans to watch TV on Thursday night. Obviously, I just never quite understand the concept that ex-boyfriends are ex-boyfriends for a reason.

— Nina, 25

I've been there. You've been there. We've all been there—especially if you've been single for a while.

You haven't had a date in months—haven't laid eyes on anyone you find even remotely attractive. This toxic cocktail of three parts nasty dry spell and one part penchant for glorifying the past leaves you extremely vulnerable to your ex-boyfriend's "Let's give it one more try" proposition. Bam! Before you know it, you're back in the fray—the ex-fray.

Of course, you have your reasons. Some of which are halfway legit. Maybe you live in a small town with a shallow pool of eligible bachelors or you tend to have a hard time working your ex-boyfriends out of your system or you're just flat out lonely. Whatever the explanation, the outcome remains the same—a revolving door approach to relationships keeping you in an on-again/off-again holding pattern.

You've heard the definition of insanity, right? "Doing the same thing over and over and expecting different results." Interestingly, both Ben Franklin and Albert Einstein receive credit for coining the maxim but I would have sworn the quote came from a single woman burned repeatedly by forays into the ex-fray.

One more quote for you: "As a dog that returns to his vomit, so is a fool who repeats his folly." Sorry about the vulgar imagery, but I'm trying to make a point. And at some level you know it—because though you try to convince yourself it'll be different this time, you can't completely stifle the little voice inside asking, *if we didn't work out before, what do we have going for us now*? Will the second (or third or fourth) time be the charm? Really? How?

Naturally, as a veteran girl-about-town, you've likely been on both sides of this story. You've broken up with boyfriends, but then panicked and begged them back within the week. Next time around you got the heave-ho, but a month later answered the phone to a "My bad! Can we try again?" And sure, we're drawn to the romantic notion that stars might uncross and stabilize a previously shaky relationship, but do we *really* believe it?

Furthermore, let's look at the cold, hard facts. I hate to be the one to remind you, but if your ex did the breaking up, he decided to *improve* his life by *removing* you. Remember that. Keep it prominent in your mind. He had you and let you go. He risked never laying eyes on you again. Period. So what's his explanation for wanting you back so badly now? Did the girl he dumped you for return the favor? Has he decided to quit searching for the love of his life and settle for you? That sounds promising.

Similarly, if you broke up with him, you need to recall the circumstances that incited your exit and consider any underlying motivations for reuniting. Do you truly want him back or are you just tired of dateless Saturday nights? Did the flame really rekindle or has your hope expired and you figure he'll do?

Granted, if enough time has passed and your ex has demonstrated significant growth and maturity—and by that I mean he finally made good on his promise to check into rehab or he underwent six years of psychoanalysis or he attended so many anger management workshops he developed his own curriculum and now teaches the courses himself at the local community college—then yes, by all means, the potential for a new and improved relationship exists. Very exciting! *You and Your Man 2.0* holds boundless possibilities!

But unless some major changes have occurred, the prognosis for this go round fares no better than the last six times you took a crack at it. You'll keep forcing the relationship *again*, smashing that square peg into a round hole *again*. And inadvertently, you'll set you both up for some wicked heartache *again*.

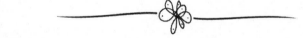

PSYCH 101: WHY WE DO IT

Oh, it makes perfect sense. You're so comfortable with him. It feels so familiar. You know exactly what you'd be getting into. In so many ways, going back to your ex provides the perfect solution—a welcome relief from the strain of the single lifestyle. No more anxious first date jitters. No more boring yourself to tears rattling off your résumé and vital stats to three new guys in one week. You can hit the club and just enjoy your girls, free of the pressure to keep one eye peeled for your next boyfriend.

Plus, of all the toads you kissed in your stint back "out there", not one turned into anything remotely regal, though you did manage to meet several court jesters, trolls, and hobbits along the way. After trudging through this ogre-laden Enchanted Forest, your ex starts looking better and better. Maybe you were wrong to let him go. What was all the fuss about, anyway? You probably blew things way out of proportion. Sure he was possessive, controlling, petty, irrational, insensitive, uncouth, and obstinate—but in the most charming way. And hey, maybe he is kind of a jerk, but he's *your* jerk.

Such agile arguments and cogent justifications often serve as sufficient ammunition to usher us back into the arms of an ex. No judgment here. It's completely understandable. Enduring months (or years) of first date disappointment saps our energy and dampens our spirits. We get really darn tired.

Then the doubts set in. Maybe what we had was as good as it gets. We keep seeking a better match, anticipating an upgrade to a snazzier model, but what if we've been driving the top of the line all along? Our dreams of a superior relationship might be just that— dreams.

Ultimately, this final rationale may prove the most persuasive of all. Not that we would ever *intend* to settle, but after a prolonged stint of being single we begin to lose faith. We convince ourselves that fairy tales don't come true, and we might as well find someone we can be reasonably happy with and call it quits. And though he came with plenty of foibles, your ex made you—well, maybe not quite *happy*, but content. So why not give it another chance?

Furthermore, as we look around and witness the adultery, abuse, and apathy infesting our friends' marriages, we question the logic in waiting for The One. Even if we meet the perfect boyfriend, won't he, too, eventually morph into the inconsiderate, ungrateful, insensitive creature known as a husband? Is there really such a thing as Mr. Right? Your best friend thought she had him, yet her husband recently confessed to an affair and filed for divorce. A coworker tied the knot last year, but spends every lunch hour badmouthing the man she basically dragged down the aisle. And you certainly can't remember the last time your book club discussed character development or Biblical allusions. No time for such literary discourse— it would cut into the husband bashing.

We start to think, *If I'm going to be miserable in five years anyway, what's the point of holding out for any particular man? If all guys are about the same, I guess my ex-boyfriend isn't such a bad choice.*

It just hasn't happened yet

I get it, yet I can't support it. And trust me, I've seen it time and time again. Women approach their "scary age" and if no man appears on the horizon, they start scrolling through their contacts, ready to rustle up a tolerable-enough ex. Memories of arguments and deal breakers pale in comparison to the thought of showing up solo to Great Aunt Enid's Christmas dinner for the sixth year running.

But I just can't condone returning to the past when the future could be brighter than you can possibly imagine! A wonderful relationship might be coming your way next month, next week, or even tomorrow. To cave and settle for an ex at this point makes no sense whatsoever, especially since you've already made it through the hardest part—the break up and recovery!

Admittedly, some couples have success when giving it another go. And if such a story line lies in your future, more power to you. But if your desire to reconnect with your ex-boyfriend reflects fatigue and I'll-never-find-a-decent-husband hopelessness, you need a motivational seminar and a shot of caffeine, not a reunification with a former flame.

Sure, marriage is risky business and many husbands stink! They take their wives for granted, grow pot bellies, and amuse themselves in the sack with Dutch Ovens (you know, the thing with the flatulence under the covers... ugh!). But for every dud husband, there's a stud husband. And don't you think the chance of a happy marriage increases if you enter the union with someone who excites, thrills, and stimulates you as opposed to someone you dredged up when rummaging through the skeletons in your closet?

Ditto

Dr. Laura Berman, Assistant Clinical Professor of Psychiatry at Northwestern University and world-renowned radio and TV relationship expert, offers the following suggestions for breaking bad ex-boyfriend habits:

"Change your pattern. When relationships get stuck in a revolving rut, it is generally because our lives are stuck in a revolving rut. By changing your routine, you can change your point of view and end a make-up and break-up cycle... It might be helpful to keep two lists on hand with you at all times—one list to remind you why the relationship can't work (he doesn't want kids, you don't share similar life goals, etc.), and one list to remind you why you are content and complete as you are (you love the freedom to meet new people, you have a wonderful network of friends and family, etc.)."[18]

Girl Talk

Dear Karin,

Don't you think you're making a really big deal out of nothing? What's your beef with the whole getting back with your ex-boyfriend thing? And by the way, for someone who's usually so positive, you're being really negative here. I mean, you act like people can never get it right once there's been a break-up in their history. Everyone knows that sometimes it takes a while for a couple to work out the kinks. Why would you insist they shouldn't give it a try when this time it might finally work out for them?

So let me take a stab at a little Psych 101 myself. Is this possibly your issue? Were you so horribly traumatized after going around and around with an ex-boyfriend that now you make these big generalizations about the futility of it all? If that's the case, I feel bad for you, of course, but it's not fair to assume that no other couple will be able to get it together just because you guys couldn't.

— Tiffany, 25

Dear Tiffany,

Okay, I'll admit, this topic is a live one for me. I've certainly never managed a clean break with a guy. Every romantic relationship I've ever had has meandered around in the gray area between together and broken up for *at least* several months after the initial split. And the times I've officially reunited with an ex haven't felt so good and never worked out.

Maybe you're onto something—I might be coming down a little hard on this because I've never gotten it right myself. Good analysis. Were you a psych major, too?

That being said, I still stand by the points I made in the chapter—especially the idea of holding out for a better fit rather than settling for an ex just because you're so dang weary of dating. Of course you're tired. But you're going to be much more tired trapped in an uninspiring marriage!

I'm just going to say it—in many cases, returning to an ex amounts to settling. And you know how I feel about *that*!

— Karin

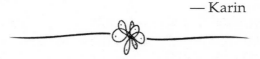

The Awful Truth

Remember, these scenes are not *based* on real stories. They *are* real stories!

ONE MORE TIME, WITH FEELING

CAST.

CASSIE: 29-years-old, recently engaged to her on-again/off-again boyfriend of 5 years, Rod, a high school math teacher and soccer coach

LORRAINE: Cassie's best friend and roommate

INTERIOR — THE WOMEN'S APARTMENT — DAY

Cassie and Lorraine are in the middle of a heated argument.

> LORRAINE
>
> There's NO WAY you just got engaged to Rod! This is completely absurd, Cassie! You guys have been in this back-and-forth relationship for years! And now you've been back together for like 10 minutes and you think it makes sense to get married? Do you see how nutty that is?

> CASSIE
>
> This is *so* not what I need from you right now, Lorraine. As my best friend, you should be happy for me. I always support you in your relationships!

LORRAINE
Because I don't date jerks, Cassie! You have good reason to support me and I have good reason to NOT support you! You've said yourself that Rod doesn't treat you right!

CASSIE
But I still keep going back to him, don't I?

LORRAINE
Because you're crazy.

CASSIE
Because I love him, Lorraine. And yeah, we've had our problems and yeah, we fight. But at some point in your life you realize maybe it's not so much about finding someone you can live with, but finding someone you can't live without.

Lorraine shakes her head, unconvinced.

LORRAINE
Or maybe it's just you're 29 and you're terrified of being single at 30.

161

Fast-forward five years:
Cassie and Rod are divorced. Cassie is raising their daughter alone because Rod ran off with a high school senior.

Lesson learned: Admittedly, this is an extreme example and the vast majority of our on-again/off-again boyfriends aren't latent pedophiles. Still, it's a good reminder that if you and your man keep breaking up, your relationship is, well, broken. You may not even be able to put your finger on why, but maybe you should trust the natural course of events—you quite possibly may have dodged a bullet. Just walk away.

Guy Talk

So here's where I'm gonna completely disagree with Karin because—well, she's wrong. And I'm not trying to tick her off or anything because she's the one paying me (and by that I mean she's buying me a lot of beer) and I'm sure that when she asked me to provide a guy's perspective, she didn't expect me to challenge her every assertion. But here goes...

First of all, I'm a little surprised with her take on this subject because she's doing that infuriating thing so many women do—talking about guys as if we're all the same—and saying that in all cases and at all times, it's a bad idea to get back with an ex-boyfriend because if it didn't work out the first time, it'll never work out during round two. She's basically assuming all guys are fools and none of us should ever be given a second chance. Is she kidding? That just doesn't make sense.

I mean, how can she possibly advise you to never ever go back with an ex? She doesn't know the 411 on your relationships. Besides, timing is everything! I know plenty of couples who split up for a while—he needed time to find himself via a backpacking trip through Europe, or she couldn't see the relationship clearly till she signed up for a clairvoyance certification program in Sedona—but once these individual pursuits were resolved, they came back together and ended up really happy.

That's not to say some guys don't intentionally use lame reasons to take a sabbatical from a relationship and then saunter on back when they're a) lonely, b) bored, or c) lookin' for some lovin'. They might serve up all sorts of lines— "I'm commitment phobic," or "I've got to get some stuff out of my system," or "I need to do this on my own, baby." And yeah, in some cases it's complete B.S. But there are also some really nice guys out there who do, in fact, have some instability or immaturity going on and mean it when they give those sorts of explanations. Did you ever think about that, Karin?

Besides, this whole book is a statement against the generalities and assumptions people make about single women, yet you're doing the exact same thing about single men, assuming they're all trying to win you back just to hurt you again.

And another point Karin fails to make—women do this, too. For example, I have this one friend who left her boyfriend to get back with an ex and then left the ex to get back with the other ex, who she eventually married. Okay, that was really confusing, but the point is, she had to jump in the ring for another round with both ex-boyfriends before her decision became clear. What would Karin have to say about that, huh? (Um, Guy, I know Maria, too. I'm aware of her story. And what I have to say about it is—) **It's not your turn, Karin...** (But you asked!) **It was rhetorical, and you know it!** (Okay, okay. Carry on. — Karin)

My point is, maybe it wasn't pretty, but Maria needed to go through that mess in order to figure it all out. And it's unfortunate that the bachelors got jerked

around and that one came up empty handed but hey, what's the expression? All's fair in love and war...

— Guy

Wow! He had a lot to say about that one, didn't he? I can't figure out if he made a decent argument or if he was just trying to make us feel sorry for all his emotionally unstable friends so we'd give them another chance.

Maybe we're not even disagreeing so much here. Really, it's more about *why* you're getting back with your ex. If you've given up and you're settling, then I stand my ground, but if you've both grown and changed and you've still got the hots for each other, then who am I to stand in your way? Ultimately, this is a complex issue and, hey, now you've got two perspectives to consider and you can decide for yourself. You're a big girl after all.

— Karin

Selfie

Admittedly, I recycled more than a few relationships in my day.

It started with my first boyfriend in college, Eddie, who broke up with me after a year but quickly changed his mind and begged me to give him another chance. I agreed and we dated for a few more months but the damage had been done and we parted ways when he graduated at the end of my sophomore year.

Next up was Kyle and I've already told you about our three year on again/off again saga. Not only did we toggle between dating and breaking up but even during our off-again periods we acted like we were together which confused everyone, including us.

However, my most egregious violation of everything I espouse in this chapter occurred with Dylan. We dated for two years but broke up when he made good on his long-term goal to move to New York. I remained in Chicago and despite the distance we kept pseudo-dating for the next four years. Giving six years of your thirties to a dead-end relationship isn't the smartest move for a woman who wants to marry and have a family, but that's exactly what I did.

So yeah, I guess Tiffany nailed it. This chapter came from literally years of agonizing personal experience. Guilty.

I remember something my friend's mom once said when we were in our twenties. We were girl talking over dinner about our inability to get guys out of our system. She leaned in and said, "Which is more painful? To cleanly sever something in one swift slice or slowly lacerate it, tearing away shred after shred with the dullest knife you can find?" Sadly, I tended to opt for the latter and I utterly regret it.

In fact, if there were one thing I could change about how I handled my 27 years of dating it would be my unwillingness to make clean breaks. I wish I'd read this chapter before I wrote it—which I understand is impossible, but you get what I mean. I could have saved myself an enormous amount of emotional torment if I'd let "No" be my final answer—especially when my exes posed the proverbial "Can we still be friends?"

Shout Out!

So to my smart, sexy, savvy, singletons I say this: You can't teach an old boyfriend new tricks and why would you want to anyway? The ex-fray keeps you mired in a murky past; wouldn't it be nice to leave the scars and heartache behind and make a fresh start with someone new? But to step into your promising future you need to fly solo for a while. Which is a great idea anyway... because single is the new black.

chapter 10

Stop Thinking About It So Much!

a mind is a terrible thing to waste

A thing I've realized after dating some really-bad-for-me guys is that once we broke up, I was always analyzing myself, trying to figure out what I was doing wrong when, in reality, I was just dating guys that weren't right for me. Now with my current boyfriend I never overanalyze or second guess myself because he likes me the way I am.

— Katrina, 27

Although women have the reputation of being overly emotional, we're in our heads quite a bit, too. Not that we're necessarily doing anything useful up there. It's often a toss-up between predicting the long-term potential of Bachelor #47 or rehashing the demise of our last five relationships. Or, to be a bit more precise, we're obsessing, ruminating and cogitating about men. And most of the time, it ain't pretty.

Bluntly put, most single women think about men—a lot. Many of us spend as much time analyzing guys as we do engaging in other hobbies and interests—especially considering these extracurricular activities often serve as oblique platforms for talking about men anyway.

Even the term *girl talk* is a misnomer and you know it. Who are we kidding? It would be way more appropriate to call it *guy talk*. The topic *du jour* at Sunday brunch? Guys! Discussions over martinis and manicures? Guys! Our weekly phone call to mom? Admit it—guys!

Granted, talking about men is, for most single women, essentially a form of entertainment. But is it really all that fun?

Well, sure, some parts of it are a lot of fun and even serve an essential purpose. Conversation constitutes the foundation of female friendships. It distinguishes us from the testosterone-drenched half of our species. Guys shoot hoops, quail, and shots, whereas chicks chitchat. And true, men shoot the breeze occasionally, too, but these airy discussions usually involve debating who's the all-time best catcher (Johnny Bench, obviously!) or the advantages of canned vs. bottled beer (no comment, I'm not a beer drinker). Women's heart-to-hearts, on the other hand, relay relationship advice, detail dating dilemmas, and bolster bruised egos. Each feminine exchange solidifies our attachments, deepening their significance.

So though I'm hesitant to censure a revered ritual intrinsic to American womanhood, I submit we might consider better topics to monopolize our neural activity. "Better" because talking about men is hardly a benign pastime. Quite the opposite, it subtly and sneakily demoralizes and demeans us. In all actuality, obsessing about men and overanalyzing our relationships gets us absolutely nowhere and fails to improve our love lives one whit. And the most damaging part—it keeps us fixated on unavailing cogitation. We just keep spinning our wheels.

Well, now I sound like a killjoy and maybe just a bit paranoid, too...

But hear me out. We've already discussed the dangers of focusing on that which we can't change (see Chapter 1). And we've refuted the faulty logic of trying to control the uncontrollable with a self-deprecating method of dreaming up some flaw that, once fixed, will usher in Mr. Right. Not helpful.

Still another problem with thinking too much about guys and rehashing our relationships (or lack thereof) is that it prevents us from appreciating all the fantastic things going on in our lives *now*. We ignore our good health, our fabulous friends, our stimulating jobs, and our rapidly improving tennis game. We dismiss all this and exist in limbo, acting as if our lives won't actually begin until we secure a serious relationship. What a waste of a fab life!

Furthermore, some of us waste not only our fabulous lives but also our fabulous selves. All the appraising, dissecting, and ruminating prompt unwarranted doubts and propel us, at times, to alter who we are. How many times have you and your girlfriends run through the post-date play-by-play, analyzing each conversational exchange and behavioral nuance? Does this sound familiar? "Okay, Clare, here's what happened. We were talking about next weekend and I said I didn't care if we went to his sister's party or not. Then he seemed to get quiet... Maybe that wasn't the right thing to say. I probably sounded kind of aloof. I bet that's why he hasn't called yet. But I didn't want to look too eager to meet his family. Everyone says you have to play it cool, right? And then when we were talking about the HIV epidemic in sub-Saharan Africa, I kept going on and on about the ONE Campaign. But he didn't have much to say about that, either. He probably got sick and tired of my proselytizing, right? Great, now he thinks I'm pushy, opinionated and that I hate his entire family!"

Are you kidding? The guy's reaction probably had absolutely nothing to do with the content of the conversation or his date's opinions. More than likely he just didn't have anything else to say. Yet she interprets his silence as a rejection of core elements of herself—her beliefs and perspectives. And to make matters worse, based on her spurious explanation she begins to adjust her conduct to align with what she incorrectly believes to be her man's preferences. What a racket! And wrong on so many levels! Yet we do it all the time.

Please, if you've got charisma and verve and cogent arguments to articulate, you better keep hopping up on soapboxes and spouting your spiel. It's the essence of who you are and what you're about. Besides, changing for a guy is super lame. And it's a tragic waste of a fabulous mind and a fabulous self.

Psych 101: why we do it

We're still trapped, really—caught in visceral understandings of our purpose and worth. Women remain excessively concerned with romantic relationships because, for the last few millennia, our very survival depended on securing a husband. And though our existence no longer requires such subjection, we still function within a culture whose gender norms derive from persistent, primordial survival instincts. And unfortunately, these prove almost impossible to shake.

So despite the fact we don't need a man, most of us want one—badly. And when we don't have one, we feel it—badly.

In addition, our enculturation has done a thorough and exhaustive job leaving us feeling incomplete and inept without a guy. And who wants to feel incomplete and inept? So begins the pondering, obsessing, and ruminating. If we just give it enough deliberation, sufficient brain power, we'll surely figure out which hang-up tanked our last relationship or bring to light any subconscious barriers blocking us from finding a good man in the first place. We're smart women, after all! It can't be all that difficult.

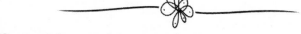

It just hasn't happened yet

Analyzing your man and your love life *ad nauseum* gets you nowhere. Strategizing, maneuvering, and gauging prove futile because if your relationship is meant to happen, it will. Frankly, if it's right, you can break every rule, mess up every move, never giving it a second thought, and it'll still work out—because it's right.

Take, for example, my friend, Erica. Erica met Matt at Molly's party. They hit it off right away—joked, laughed, and had a great time. Molly later told Erica that Matt's post-party recap contained a resounding, "Erica rocks!" But Erica didn't hear from Matt. He knew Molly had Erica's number, had already acknowledged an interest in Erica, yet never bothered to get her number. So Erica called Matt instead. Oops! Mistake #1.

Mistake #2 quickly followed because after a few minutes of chatting on the phone, Erica asked Matt out on a date. That weekend they went out for drinks and dinner and had a fantastic time—so much so that Erica proceeded to Mistake #3—she slept with Matt on the first date.

And did he call the next day? No. So she called him—Mistake #4. Hang tight. It gets better. After six months of dating, Erica suggested Matt move in with her, since he was living in his parents' basement—Mistake #5. A year later, Erica explained to Matt that she was nearing thirty and it would be a good time for him to think about proposing. *All together now*—Mistake #6! So he popped the question. Today Erica and Matt are happily married with three beautiful sons.

Obviously, Erica didn't spend too much time thinking about her game plan. She did it *all* wrong but it turned out *all* right. Because it *was* right.

Ditto

The over-analyzing epidemic has reached a global scale. Apparently, our sisters across the Atlantic possess a similar propensity for excessive scrutinizing of verbal (and digital) exchanges, as evidenced by the musings of British blogger, Natalie Lue:

"We've all been there. Boy meets girl. They have a great time in the honeymoon period, but the girl just has to analyze every phone call, every text, every email and everything that comes out of his mouth. Sometimes I blame technology because the lazy communication that texts and emails yield means that we can interpret stuff whatever way we want to.

Women are supposed to be far more emotional creatures than men and this is great, however we burn up too much brain power obsessing over things that could do with being put on the back burner."[19]

On this side of the pond, writer Lauren Martin echoes this sentiment. "There's no one to blame for our misery and disillusionment but ourselves. Because that exhausting, all-consuming, life-destroying over-analyzing that's slowly killing us, that's all on us."

She goes on to chastise women not only for compulsive dissection of texts received and sent, but also for ruminating over those texts that never come—"So, he hasn't texted you in three days. Either he's not into you, he's a horrible texter or he lost his phone. Either way it's not your problem. Sitting around wondering what your empty screen means is getting you nowhere. What it means is that you need to move on and start finding other hobbies besides anticipating blinking lights and vibrations."[20]

Girl Talk

Dear Karin,

Well, first of all, you're <u>so</u> the pot calling the kettle here. I mean, this entire book is devoted to staying true to yourself and how to be cool going it alone until the right guy comes along. But aren't we pretty much obsessing about guys in each and every chapter?

Now in a way, I agree with you. We really should talk about other stuff—especially since it's ridiculous how we spend hours asking our girlfriends to help us figure out what guys are thinking. But do we ever go straight to the source? No! Then we read all those self-help books claiming to illuminate the male mind, but the catch is the authors are all women. How's that for the blind leading the blind?

But in another way, I don't agree with you. We absolutely learn important things about relationships by processing with our girlfriends. We examine our girlfriend's mistake and make different choices, or we see she's having a hard time with her man so we steer clear of that type of guy. There's got to be some value in it or else we wouldn't do it so much right?

So, I think you should relax a bit and stop raining on our girl talk—I mean, guy talk—parade!

— Becky, 28

Dear Becky,

Okay. I hear you and I should admit upfront that I felt a little uncomfortable writing this chapter. Clearly, I've spent a ton of time pondering this subject myself—so much so that I wrote a book on it. Yet now I'm trying to tell you to quit obsessing about a topic in which I've immersed myself for the last several years. Hypocrite!

But that's the point. I'm hoping this book will help us all stop thinking so much about our man-less status—or at least think about it differently.

We need to diligently correct our thoughts when we slip up—those times when we worry, "Maybe there is something wrong with me"—and resist buying into society's "marriage-at-all-costs" mandate and check lingering faulty cognition and skewed reasoning, *i.e.* "If I just do _____, he'll show up..."

Squandered genius! Frittered brilliance! No more desecrating precious neural energy on trivialities!

I know, I know. I'm hopping off the soapbox now.

— Karin

The Awful Truth

Remember, these scenes are not *based* on real stories. They *are* real stories!

MISTY WATER-COLORED FIXATIONS

CAST.
MEGHAN: 35-year-old corporate attorney
HILLARY: her new coworker, who just started
    at the firm

INTERIOR — DOWNTOWN BAR — NIGHT

It's Friday evening and the women are enjoying an after-work cocktail. They've just recently met and are getting to know each other, as women often do, by talking about their love lives. Meghan has been prattling on about a failed relationship for the past 20 minutes.

> MEGHAN
> ...so as for Jimmy, I've never really been able to figure out why we only made it a few months— although my friend Dana said it was because I was putting closure on my relationship with my last boyfriend, Corey, by trying to "work it out" with my next boyfriend. And since Jimmy was the next guy I dated after Corey, I ended up dragging along all my Corey-baggage, you know what I mean? Almost like how girls with

absentee dads will keep dating guys who can't commit because it's like if they can get some guy to stick around it will somehow make up for the fact that their dads were never there for them. I don't know if that's really what I was doing, but that was Dana's take on it, you know?

HILLARY
Wow.   It   sounds   like   that relationship really did a number on you.

MEGHAN
Oh yeah, for sure.

HILLARY
How serious were you? Were you talking marriage?

MEGHAN
Oh, my gosh, no!   Jimmy and I dated in high school!

Lesson Learned: We can waste a lot of time and energy psychoanalyzing ancient history.   Don't we have anything better to do? As long as we're consumed by the past, we fail to step into our bright future! Let's get to it!

Guy Talk

Wow. This chapter is a real window into Chick World. So you women just talk about men all day, every day? Man, I wish I'd known this little gem a long time ago. But at the same time, when it comes to this subject, it's funny, because in a way we're really not all that different. True, on any given Sunday afternoon, guys are talking smack while playing pick-up basketball, not complaining about their lady troubles over brunch. But trust me, the sports are just a cover up. Guys obsess about women plenty. We just don't 'fess up to it as much—definitely not to each other and maybe not even to ourselves.

And I'm not saying that our way is the healthiest approach either, but guys are in a rough spot with this stuff. Society dictates confining expectations for men, too you know. I mean, we're supposed to be tough and hard—a "man's man"—and if we show any weakness or sensitivity we're considered pansies or sissies. So, we're not too apt to start crying in our beer when we're out with the boys or even when we're out with you. Because, although you women say you want us to communicate and express our emotions, sometimes it bites us in the butt.

Take, for example, my friend Jay. He dated Renée for about six months, during which time she constantly pined for her ex-boyfriend, a rugged, tough-guy construction worker from New Zealand. Jay, a writer and musician, is a more artistic guy and initially Renée loved his sensitivity—especially as he played therapist trying to repair her broken heart. But eventually the novelty of his "emo" vibe wore off and Renée started making cracks about his sexuality. When he wore a turtle neck sweater, she called him "femmy". When he couldn't figure out how to put wheel covers on her car, she ridiculed. When he flubbed up the assembly of her new Ikea bookcase well, what kind of man was he anyway? All this plus an incessant need to talk about their relationship? He had to be gay!

And you know how sexy it makes a guy feel when his girlfriend accuses him of being gay. Yeah, they didn't last too long after that.

But back to the point. We think a lot about women, too. We might not talk about it—because, as

Jay's situation pointed out, that can backfire—but we think about you.

— Guy

Well, it feels good to know men obsess about us sometimes as well. And from the way Guy puts it, they have it worse because at least chick culture permits us to dish about men and talk about our feelings without having anyone question our sexuality. See, we women can be horrible about this stuff! We beg and plead guys to "open up" and share what they're feeling. Then when they do, we hit 'em with the "don't be such a wuss!" bit. Not nice, ladies. Not nice at all.

— Karin

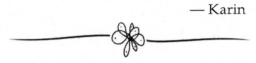

Selfie

I used to get so irritated with myself for obsessing about relationships all the time.

Yes, I had a full life. Yes, I was making progress in my career. Yes, I lived in a hip neighborhood in a fantastic city. Yes, I had strong, meaningful friendships.

I knew how good I had it and I was very thankful for the many amazing aspects of my life. But I still wanted to find love and it caused me to think about guys more than I wanted to.

But I wasn't the only one. All my single girlfriends had the same problem and it drove us nuts! And since every woman we knew suffered from this annoying ailment, we figured we could probably blame it on some sort of biological mandate inherent to female neurology.

Though our theory has yet to be tested, we're sticking to it.

Here goes—the female brain will constantly think about a guy due to a neurological mechanism known as the Boy Void. The neurons of the Boy Void are designed to continually hurl a man's name into a woman's stream of consciousness, ostensibly for the purpose of procreation.

This explains a phenomenon commonly noted in the cognitive processes of single women—one my friends and I experienced regularly. If a woman lacks prospects on the dating front, her Boy Void will dip into her "ex-files" and conjure up a former boyfriend to ponder. *I wonder what's up with Mike? Maybe we could make another go of it. We got along pretty well. I think our timing was just off...* Or she'll entertain the idea of accepting her upstairs neighbor's open-ended invitation to grab coffee sometime even though she finds him physically unattractive and a bit kooky. Or she'll obsess about the boy she rejected in 10th grade wondering if she made a huge mistake refusing to go to prom with him two years in a row.

You get the picture. In fact, if you're anything like my girlfriends and me, you've been there done that. And now, thanks to us, you realize you have an overactive Boy Void to blame. You're welcome.

Shout Out!

So to my smart, sexy, savvy, singletons I say this: Let's find new subject matter for Girl Talk and give our armchair psychologists a break. Besides, a mind is a terrible thing to waste—especially one as whip smart as yours! The overanalyzing proves fruitless anyway because we already know why you're single—it just hasn't happened yet! Which is perfectly fine... because single is the new black.

chapter 11

Quit Worrying About Being Alone Forever!

fear is a powerful thing

I think if I knew that at the end of all this I'd definitely find someone, I'd be okay. I could relax and enjoy my time as a single woman. But deep down, I worry I'll be alone forever. And I have two cats, so there's that.

— Kasey, 24

Here's the tragic reality—women make *a slew* of horrible, soul crushing mistakes out of fear of being alone.

Our desire for connection and intimacy isn't the problem—that's perfectly normal. Moreover, psychologists highlight mental and physical benefits related to strong attachments and note that the healthiest among us enjoy a robust network of social support. The urge to bond is likely a hardwired fixture inherent to the human condition.[21] Most of us crave relationship with a life partner, someone with whom to share our journey.

But sometimes our yearnings for intimacy take

precedence over good sense and reason. We elevate connection to the extent we dread its antithesis—solitude. We become excessively scared of being alone.

That's where the problem sets in—because when we're afraid, we relinquish an enormous amount of personal agency and power. Cowering to anxiety, we let panic cloud our decision making. We reason it's better to be in a relationship—any relationship—than to be alone. Even if said relationship crushes your spirit and robs you of *you*. We deny our true desires and lose sense of our authentic selves. In essence, we live phony lives.

And then we do some really stupid stuff.

We date guys we know aren't good for us—or ones we don't even like that much. We remain in dysfunctional and abusive relationships. We take back cheating boyfriends. We pretend to be in love. We marry the wrong guy. We stay married to the wrong guy. We have affairs. We get divorced but rush into another marriage with the same screwed up dynamics.

We create colossal chaos, leaving a dysfunctional legacy to our children, if we have any, just to keep from being alone—because we deem it so utterly intolerable.

PSYCH 101: WHY WE DO IT

So what gives? Why do we fear being alone to

the point of making massive messes of our lives? Because we attach a great deal of *meaning* to it.

We buy into the fallacy that being alone means three objectionable things:

1) *I'm alone because I'm unlovable,*

2) *I'm alone because no one wants me* and

3) *Since I'm alone now, I'll be alone forever.*

All three are flat out lies that will cripple you emotionally and destroy your love life if you subscribe to them.

Let me take a moment to break these down starting with *I'm alone because I'm unlovable.* Too often single women measure their lovability by the presence of a male in their lives. And yes, it feels fantastic when a wonderful man is madly in love with us. There's no denying it.

But if we find ourselves "manless" for a season, does it make any sense whatsoever to conclude we've all of a sudden become unlovable? What sort of logic is that?

Do we have friends who love us? Yes. Do we have family members who love us? Yes. Do we have coworkers and associates who love us? Yes and yes. Well since these folks adore us with or without a man in tow, then inarguably, we remain lovable. Your lovability doesn't break down with every break up. It just doesn't work that way.

So unless you have absolutely no trace of love in your life (and if that's the case, I'd highly recommend you find a great therapist to help you develop social skills and learn how to bond with others) then you're still lovable *sans* man.

On to the next notion—*I'm alone because no one wants me.* Let's face it, this one could be true—at this particular time, in the circles in which you run, no man may want you.

But again, we need to appeal to logic. It's simply preposterous to assume that because no one you currently interact with cares to date you, that all other men on planet Earth are disinterested as well. A much more plausible explanation for your single status is this: plenty of men would be into you—and will be into you—once they have the chance to meet you.

And let's not forget, you don't want 99% of the men in your scene either. Yet your disinterest doesn't make them worthless or undesirable as partners. They're just not the guys for you. Similarly, it's illogical to conclude that because every bachelor in your office hasn't professed undying love means you're worthless and undesirable.

As for the third lie—*Since I'm alone now I'll be alone forever*—well, it's utterly irrational.

You don't know the future. You have no idea who you'll run into tomorrow or who you might meet next month. Besides, statistics are on your side since the majority of Americans marry. According to National Center of Health Statistics, "the probability that men will marry by age 40 is 81%; for women, it is 86%."[22] Moreover, these numbers don't factor in those people who find life partners but prefer not to marry.

It just hasn't happened yet

Now that we understand the absurdity of our fear, we have no excuse but to do something about it. As Maya Angelou said, "Do the best you can until you know better. Then when you know better, do better." So let's do better!

To help with this, I want to teach you a quick, but profound, trick from cognitive therapy. I'm borrowing from the work of one of my favorite psychologists, Dr. Albert Ellis, founder of Rational Emotive Behavior Therapy (REBT). Ellis encourages us to examine and, when needed, contest our thoughts through questioning, reasoning, and logic—a technique he calls "cognitive disputations".[23]

Through disputing our cognitions we challenge the *meaning* we attribute to an event/situation/circumstance, which changes our thoughts about it and thus changes our emotions.

Here's how to work "cognitive disputations". First, we pay close attention to our thoughts so we can recognize when unreasonable ones sneak in. Then, when we identify an irrational thought, we dismantle it the way I did earlier in the chapter.

Let's practice with the following example:

Irrational Belief: *I haven't had a boyfriend in two years. I'm such a loser. I'm so depressed.*

Cognitive Disputation: *How does being single equate to being a loser? That's irrational! As a matter of fact, being alone takes guts! I've been strong and brave and taken care of myself. I've also refused to settle—which makes me the exact <u>opposite</u> of a loser. There's no reason to be depressed because being alone doesn't <u>mean</u> anything unless I <u>decide</u> it does.*

And by the way, this isn't just some warm-fuzzy exercise in psychobabble—an enormous amount of research in cognitive therapy substantiates the effectiveness of REBT.

Ditto

In her book *Choosing Me Before We*, Christine Arylo underscores the theme of this chapter, urging women to learn to meet their own emotional needs and embrace the self-discovery solitude affords.

Arylo recalls irrational beliefs she held when single—that "only two men (my fiancé and a previous boyfriend) will ever really love me. I was convinced that, if one of these two guys was not my soul mate, then I'd be alone forever, and being alone was a fate worse than death."

When her engagement collapsed, she finally appreciated the benefits of solitude, "The Truth, with a capital *T*, is that there are plenty of good men to go around. If we are having trouble finding one, let's stop blaming the numbers and start looking at ourselves. Maybe being single is the best thing for you right now... time alone is often a blessing and a big part of personal discovery. Why can't we just be okay with being on our own? Why do we get so hung up on being alone instead of embracing our solo period and learning what it has to teach us?"[24]

Findings from recent studies corroborate the theme of this chapter. Researchers at the University of Toronto found that people who fear being single are prone to "settle for less" in their romantic relationships and be more dependent on these relationships, even though they acknowledge the relationships are unsatisfying. Those who fear being alone are also less likely to breakup with a significant other even if the relationship isn't working for them. The psychologists also concluded that those who dread being single are less picky when selecting potential dating partners.[25]

Bottom line: when we fear being alone, we're way more likely to settle!

Girl Talk

Dear Karin,

I knew the self-help fluff would eventually sneak into this book! You psychologists just can't resist the Rah-Rah motivational speaker shtick!

Seriously, Karin, do you really think this little "argue with myself" technique is going to cut it? Okay, so whenever I'm depressed I'm supposed to cheer myself on with, "Girl, you're so fabulous! Don't be depressed because it's super cool to be alone!" And presto! I'll feel better?

How about you give us some real advice! And I'm not talking about this magical thinking nonsense. I've been alone for forever and I'm sick of it and even though you say I shouldn't be sad about it I am!

Please just tell me what to change about myself so I can find The One. Because everyone else is coupling up and I'm tired of standing on the sidelines feeling left out.

— Ellie

Dear Ellie,

There are plenty of self-help books that will tell you what to change so you can find The One. But this isn't that kind of book.

I'm not going to pretend to have all the answers and I certainly won't tell you to change so you can meet a guy. But I did share a powerful technique with you, one that helped me tremendously when I was single—one I still use today to combat any irrational thoughts that flow through my mind. However, I'd argue that *cognitive disputations* amount to much more than "self-help fluff" since, as I mentioned earlier, a great deal of research supports the effectiveness of cognitive therapy.

Furthermore, when treating anxiety and depression, cognitive therapy proves as effective in the short term and *more* effective in the long term when compared to anti-depressants such as Prozac, Welbutrin, and Xanax and other second generation SSRIs. So for those of us preferring to stay away from meds, cognitive therapy is a potent tool for maintaining mental health.[26]

So in that sense, I did give you some advice—guidance as to how to be happy in general, as opposed to how to snag a man.

Still, I know you're sick and tired of being alone and you want a formula for getting the guy. I'm sorry to hear how disappointed you are and how much you hate your single life. So to that end, I guess I do have another piece of advice—read the chapter again—or maybe the whole book. Seriously! Sometimes truth is hard to internalize because so many irrational messages continually bombard us so we need to a refresher. But I really think (and more importantly, the research suggests) if you take control of your thoughts, you'll feel much better.

— Karin

The Awful Truth

Remember, these scenes are not *based* on real stories. They *are* real stories!

OBSESSIVE COMPULSIVE DISASTER

CAST.
MELANIE: 48-year-old nurse
TESSA: her sister

INTERIOR — SUBURBIA — NIGHT

It's Thursday evening at Tessa's home in Middle America. The sisters are arguing.

TESSA
Do you know how ridiculous you sound, Melanie? Really, do you have any idea?

MELANIE

There you go again! Judging me,
as usual!

TESSA

This goes beyond judging, Melanie.
It's simply absurd. You're just not
thinking right and it's time to get
a grip!

MELANIE

You can't possibly understand.
You've never been alone.

TESSA

No, I haven't. And I'm sure it's
not fun but rushing into a fourth
marriage to keep from being alone
is ludicrous!

MELANIE

I'm not *rushing* into things.

TESSA

You guys have only known each
other for six months! But the
biggest issue I have is that you
started dating Ted a week after
Jack moved out.

MELANIE
So what?

TESSA
So you're terrified of being alone and you're making horrible decisions because of it! You even admitted that you don't like nursing but you wanted a job where you could work the night shift and sleep all day—so you wouldn't have to wake up and spend mornings by yourself!

MELANIE
What's wrong with that?

TESSA
What's wrong with that??? Forget it. I'm done. This conversation is going absolutely nowhere. Enjoy your fourth marriage. I'll see you when it tanks.

Lesson Learned: Better to marry the wrong guy (4 times if necessary) than be alone. Oh, and when picking a career, be sure it's one that can serve as a prophylactic to your loneliness as opposed to one you're passionate about...

Guy Talk

First of all, let's get one thing straight—guys are definitely attracted to ladies who aren't afraid to be alone. From my experience, most men are turned on by mentally and emotionally strong women. And I think we tend to treat these women better, whether we realize it or not, because independent, self-sufficient women command respect by virtue of how they carry themselves.

In general, I'd say guys are actually pretty leery of women who have a ton of ex-boyfriends, ex-fiancés, or ex-husbands. Because when we meet a chick who's jumped from relationship to relationship without any breathing room, we know we're dealing with a serial dater and then we'll start to wonder—did she really have a strong connection with all those exes or is this woman just needy?"

Now, I know earlier in the book Karin assured needy women that some guys are looking for exactly what their clinginess has to offer—and I guess that may be true—but personally, I don't want a woman who's so fixated on being in a relationship she doesn't much care who she's with—just as long as she's with someone.

And really, ladies, here's the thing I keep trying to remind you—guys aren't all that different from you. When you date someone, you want to know he thinks you're special and that's he's crazy about you, right? And you'd be upset to find out you were actually just a placeholder until someone better came along—because he wanted a plus-one for the Christmas party or whatever.

Well, guys feel the same way! We want to know we're special. (Aw, Guy, that's so sweet! —Karin) Okay, I guess I teed you up for that one, Karin.

But the point is, most guys want a partner, not a project. So a strong woman who's spent some time on her own is really appealing to us.

— Guy

Don't you love it when Guy gets all soft and vulnerable? **(Wait, so wanting my girlfriend to actually like me for *me* makes me soft and vulnerable? Whatever! —Guy).** I'm just teasing, Guy, and I appreciate your candor. Because it's important for women to remember that guys are people, too, and that in so many ways, they feel the same things we do.

— Karin

Selfie

Sometimes it takes just one conversation to change your entire perspective.

When I was 29 I took a spring break trip to California with two friends, Stephanie and Anna. We drove up and down exquisite Highway 1 taking in Monterey, Carmel-by-the-Sea, Cambria, San Simeon, San Francisco, and Napa. Enjoying stunning ocean views, dramatic cliffs, and adorable sea lions, made this one of the most fantastic vacations I'd ever been on. And we all traveled well together, which was especially cool since I'd just met Anna through Stephanie.

I'll never forget one night in our hotel in Napa, Stephanie and I fell into a gripe fest about being single. We harped on pretty much every topic—the pressure to find someone, the scarcity of decent guys, the hopelessness we felt, and the alienation of living solo in a couples' world. When would love come our way? We were tired of going it alone!

Anna remained quiet throughout our rant. Since I was just getting to know her, I wasn't sure what to make of her silence. She'd gotten married right after college and therefore hadn't spent any adult years alone. Maybe she didn't feel she had much to say on the subject. Maybe she felt sorry for us. Or maybe the whole conversation bored her. I had no idea.

When Steph and I finally paused, Anna said quietly, "You know, there's no more painful loneliness than being alone when you're with someone."

That stopped us dead in our tracks.

Anna continued, "I know you guys are lonely sometimes but I'm telling you, it's way worse to feel alone in a marriage. At least you have the chance of eventually marrying the love of your life and experiencing intimacy and a deep connection. I married Joe thinking I'd found that. But I was wrong and now it's too late. And I'm really, really lonely—all the time."

Throughout my thirties and early forties whenever I got down I would think back to Anna's words and remember that I was way better off being single and occasionally lonely, than to be stuck in a bad marriage feeling utterly alone.

Shout Out!

So to my smart, sexy, savvy single ladies I say this: Quit worrying about being alone forever! And remember, you're the one who decides what it means to be alone. How 'bout we go with—you're alone because you're strong and independent. You're alone because you refuse to settle. Those seem like some pretty solid reasons for being alone. And one more perk—being alone is très chic... since single is the new black!

chapter 12

Don't Push Yourself Too Hard, but Don't Go On Hiatus, Either!

the key word here is "balance"

It's like I'm on this seesaw. Sometimes I push myself so hard trying to find someone—I get way out of my comfort zone. But other times I just want to give up entirely. I think it might be easier to learn to accept being single rather than continue to feel vulnerable and keep getting hurt.

— Maricella, 42

Balance? Really? Amidst the chaos and pandemonium of the dating scene, you're supposed to aspire to some sort of Zen equilibrium? Right...

You know I've been there. I feel your pain. Moonlighting as your own matchmaker all these years has discouraged and demoralized you. The quest to meet The One proves more and more disheartening each time you make an effort only to come up empty handed, yet again.   To make matters worse, you incessantly fend off a blitz of questions, advice, and censure regarding the fact you're still single—which gets exhausting, especially because people seem to forget that no one wants to change your relationship status more than you! Plus it's just plain disappointing when our love lives don't play out as planned.

Thankfully, you've found a book by someone who gets it—someone who's trudged through the same trenches, someone who's endured pretty much every conceivable scenario served up by the singles' scene. Finally, an author who validates your emotions and experiences, encouraging you to stay true to yourself, remain hopeful, and never, ever settle.

So in this moment, I want you to take a deep breath, relax, and just be. Bask in the comfort of feeling understood, for once. Acknowledge your courage and strength—because it takes *a lot* of guts to go it alone. Honor your path. Be grateful for all you've learned as a single woman. Feel the pride of knowing you can take care of yourself all by yourself and though you'd *like* to be with someone you don't *need* to be with anyone. Pause. Reflect. Center. Give yourself some credit.

And then... push yourself, just a little bit.

Hear me out.

Over dinner with a good friend, I learned something about myself I hadn't recognized before. We were talking about the first edition of this book and the fact that I met my husband four months after its publication. Laura thought for a moment and said, "One thing I can say about you, Karin—you always kept looking for ways to meet guys. You never got so fed up that you entirely checked out for a couple months or a year. You just kept picking yourself up and getting back in the ring."

In retrospect, I guess that's true. As a single woman, remaining open and available to meeting someone became so habitual I didn't even realize how completely I'd integrated it into my lifestyle. It had become a natural priority, a part of my weekly routine even.

But at the same time, I refused to let it dominate. I didn't let my search to meet a great guy take precedence over the salient, tangible aspects of my life *i.e.* my friends, family, interests, and career. To do so would have demeaned all the extraordinary blessings I already enjoyed. In effect, I kept my current life at a higher priority than the pursuit of the next chapter of my life, but I paid attention to both.

That being said, when I could incorporate the two, for example, by inviting my girlfriends to a First Friday at The Museum of Contemporary Art, I'd do it. Hanging out with my friends (my current life) but doing so in a setting where we could meet men (my pursuit of the next chapter)—served as a win-win.

I didn't realize it until Laura pointed it out, but

over the years, I'd found that elusive balance. For me, it entailed fully cherishing the present while remaining proactive and positive about my future.

PSYCH 101: WHY WE DO IT

We vacillate between pushing ourselves too hard and completely throwing in the towel because we're simply trying to make happen for us what seems to have come so naturally to others. So we force ourselves to "get out there" as often as possible and feel guilty for occasionally wanting to stay home and just chill on a Saturday night. Or we head in the opposite direction and go on hiatus for six months or a year, chucking dating entirely.

In either scenario, the theme of this book reverberates; we try to control what we can't control. Some of us respond to this tension by committing to the hunt with abandon, pulling out all stops in efforts to orchestrate the desired results. *I'll utterly devote myself to finding a guy. Everything else must come secondary. Once I start taking things seriously, it'll all fall into place.*

Others get utterly fed up and recoil to lick our wounds. Our hopes shattered one too many times, we can't bear the thought of more disappointment and in attempts to manage the pain and protect ourselves from additional hurt, we raise the white flag. *I can't take any more of this! I emailed that guy for 3 ½ weeks and then he just drops off the planet with no explanation? It's so demoralizing! I'm so tired of feeling rejected. I'm done.*

It just hasn't happened yet

We've already covered the hazards of going to extremes and examined how overextending yourself can lead to severe dating burnout. So this isn't about applying pressure or whipping yourself into a frenzy and ending up miserable. Sometimes you legitimately need to press "pause." If, after 13 cruddy dates in a row, you decide to step away from the laptop and let your GottaGetAMan.com membership expire, go right ahead. Or if you're in the wake of your third bad fix-up this month, you may choose to pass when your coworker begs you to grab drinks with her brother who's in for the week from Houston.

Then again, in the pursuit of balance, you might want to give yourself a little shove now and then. Maybe consider committing to at least one "find a guy" activity per week or per month—whatever feels right for you. Taking a small step like this guarantees balance because you're neither forcing the issue, nor hibernating.

If you decide to get proactive, engage in activities you'd want to do regardless—that way, you know you'll have a great time no matter what the outcome.

Another bonus—if you choose to take steps toward meeting someone, you can bow out—guilt free—of anything that feels uncomfortable while still being able to honestly tell your mom to back off because you *are* making an effort!

Ditto

When I published the first edition of this book, I knew of no other authors who shared my philosophy. But since then, I'm happy to note some additional empowering, encouraging, stay-true-to-yourself resources have become available. Sara Eckel, author of *It's Not You: 27 (Wrong) Reasons You're Single*, describes the tension she felt when seeking balance:

"Actively searching can be soul crushing, but as we all know 'letting love come naturally'—let it find you at Pilates class or your marketing job—has serious problems too. And no matter what you do, you're always informed you're wrong, alternately urged to 'just relax' or 'get out there', depending on whichever thing you're not doing.

How do you find, as the yoga teachers say, the balance between effort and surrender? For me the strategy was: Does this make me feel empowered or just exhausted? Am I allowing my desire for the evening to go one way to spill into desperation or am I maintaining my dignity?"

And that's the best answer I can find to the *how hard should you look* question—as hard as you want to."[27]

Girl Talk

Dear Karin,

Okay, so which is it? We're pretty much done reading the book and now you switch it up? You start with, "You're great! You're fine! You're fabulous— don't change a thing!" but now you tell us, "Try hard—but not too hard! Stay positive no matter how abysmal your love life has been! And definitely don't go on hiatus for too long! Oh, and lest we forget, balance is key!"

You can't have it both ways, you know. Either I'm perfect the way I am and all I have to do is sit back, relax, and wait for my knight to ride up or I'm a wreck and I need to make some changes. And if that's the case, if there is something wrong with me, would you please use that psychology degree of yours and tell me what it is and how to fix it? I bought the book looking for some answers—give me my money's worth! Where's the step-by-step formula for getting me a man?

Just tell me what to do already! I've been in a dry spell for over a year and I'm absolutely beside myself!

— Veronica, 36

Veronica,

I hear you and I hear how very frustrated, hurt, and fatigued you are. I'm sorry. I remember feeling the same way and wondering if things would ever change. And then they did—in a big way!

But despite the fact I'm a psychologist, I'm not a fan of giving advice and telling people what to do. Furthermore, I wrote this book to provide a unique source of support for single women—a book which won't lie to you by claiming to have the magic bullet for finding Mr. Right, one that assumes there are many different types of men in the world who are looking for many different types of women—so there's no point changing yourself when there's a man looking for exactly what you have to offer.

To my mind, the best way to help my single ladies is to first and foremost, empathize with you and validate your experiences as only someone who's been there can. So that's been my primary focus. But secondly, since it finally "happened" for me, I feel I should share with you how I found love. And as I've discussed, balancing the two impulses we've covered in this chapter, proved key.

So actually, I can have it both ways—because

that's what worked for me. But if my approach doesn't feel helpful, skip it. Stay true to yourself, Veronica, and find a way to tackle the dating realm that feels right for you.

— Karin

The Awful Truth

Remember, these scenes are not *based* on real stories. They *are* real stories!

WOMAN DOWN

CAST.
JILL: 37-year-old corporate trainer
DEANA: her BFF

INTERIOR — RESTAURANT — DAY

Jill and Deana have met for brunch as they do most weekends. Eventually, the conversation turns toward the men in their lives, or the lack thereof.

JILL

So, I have an announcement to make.

DEANA

This sounds pretty serious for brunch talk...

JILL

It is serious. I'm officially swearing off men. Forever.

DEANA

We've been through this before, Jill. Yes, it's rough out there and we're both tired of the dating scene but we've got to keep trying!

JILL

You can keep trying. I'm done.

DEANA

Come on! This is nonsense.

JILL

It's not nonsense. It's my life and it's my choice and it's happening.

DEANA

You sound like a crazy person.

JILL

Maybe so. But it's even crazier to keep beating my head against the wall! It's *never* going to happen!

I'm too fat and ugly. I'm too stupid and oh, let's not forget, I'm too old. Even guys in their forties are looking for twentysomethings!

DEANA
Oh, my gosh! Stop it! Where did all this negativity come from?

JILL
Please! It's been building for like the last *twenty years*!

DEANA
You've got to stay hopeful, Jill!

JILL
Staying hopeful is exhausting. I'm done with it. I'm out.

DEANA
Okay, but you're still miserable! Giving up isn't making you happier.

JILL
Well, I was miserable trying all those years, too. Maybe happiness just isn't in the cards for me.

Lesson Learned: The singles' scene can really kick a girl when she's down. It's exhausting and demoralizing and negativity creeps in so furtively, overtaking even the strongest of us. But as Deana pointed out, throwing in the towel doesn't alleviate your despair anyway—so that's not the answer. We may not have chosen to be single, but we do choose how we react to our circumstances. Striving for balance enables us to respond to the slings and arrows of singlehood with poise and hope, as opposed to burnout and despair.

Guy Talk

Listen ladies, guys go through all this, too. We deal with the push/pull of wanting to do something about being single and wanting to just forget about it. Case in point—recently my buddy, Mike, has been bugging me to sign up for a dating service because a couple years ago he joined one and then bam—he met his wife. And yes, she's hot and yes, she's smart, and yes, I wish she had a twin, but I told him, "Listen, I don't need to pay for dates." Mike quips back with, "Right. You're not paying for dates because you never have any." Ouch.

Okay, fine. He's right. I haven't met anyone I liked in a while but it seems like a stretch to hire a firm and team of matchmakers to scour the planet just to find me someone to hang out with on Saturday nights. (That's all you're looking for, Guy? Someone to grab you a beer while you binge watch *Hard Knocks* on Saturday nights? That's your first problem! How about admitting you're ready to settle down? How about being honest about the fact that you're looking for a wife? —Karin) How about letting me finish my thoughts, Karin? (You're right. Sorry. —Karin) So, I don't know for sure why I'm so resistant to trying a dating service. Maybe it's a pride thing. Or maybe I'm just being lazy and I don't want to extend myself. Or, as Karin would put it, I'm on hiatus.

But I gotta admit Mike did find himself a fine looking woman via a dating service... Food for thought.

— Guy

See, even Guy struggles to find balance. He knows he should make an effort but clearly he needs to pursue women in ways that feel comfortable and fun for him. Otherwise, he'll show up on dates as a surly, cranky curmudgeon instead of the witty, adorable hipster we know and love. (Adorable? Hipster? Really? — Guy). Maybe Mike will eventually convince him to try that dating service or Guy will download the latest dating app and give it a go. Just remember, Guy, in order to get that girl—you know, the one grabbing you beers on Saturday night while you channel surf—you may need to crawl out of that man cave of yours to see the light of day.

— Karin

Selfie

Finding balance took me a very long time. As you know, in my twenties, I remained on-again/off-again with Kyle but made virtually no effort to connect with anyone else during the off-again periods. Why bother? No one compared to Kyle so why try to meet someone who'd inevitably disappoint?

Even when he got married and I had no choice but to move on, I still dragged my feet. My thoughts became horribly defeatist. *Some people marry the love of their life. Others don't. I messed things up with Mr. Right so I'll just have to settle for Mr. Okay. I've always been unlucky in love anyway. I should just be thankful for my friends and family and forget about romance.* I remember clearly those voices in my head, though it's hard for me to believe I ever slipped so deeply into negativity.

Near the end of my twenties, in order to make up for all those reclusive years, I swung in the other direction and made finding a guy my top priority. I joined social clubs, attended mixers, formed co-ed soccer teams, and even went on a church retreat for singles all by myself—no trusty wingman by my side. Talk about awkward! Which is how I'm sure I looked—awkward and uncomfortable, vacillating between trying too hard and disinterest because my heart wasn't in it. I pushed myself to get "out there", hoping I could coerce love to come my way.

In my thirties, all my single friends had jumped online to meet men so I decided to give it a try. But as I've mentioned, it required too much time and upset my balance—I had to neglect other aspects of my life, which I was unwilling to do. And then, in my late thirties, I finally got it right.

My dad had been bugging me to try a dating service called *It's Just Lunch*. After my painful break-up with Dylan, I figured, *You know what? Dad's right. It's time to try something different.* So in my 37th summer, I made an appointment at the Chicago branch and went in for the interview.

More to come on this story…

Shout Out!

So to my smart, sexy, savvy singletons I say this: It's all about balance. Find your middle ground—not too forced, not too lax. Your pendulum may sway back and forth a bit—but that's normal. Ultimately, it just hasn't happened yet—which is perfectly fine... because single is the new black.

Part 3

words of wisdom

chapter 13

Take It From Those
Who've Been There!

we've got proof!

When I was single I was completely convinced my "intimacy issues" were just too huge and insurmountable and that I would have to be happy with my girlfriends and family and resign myself to never having a romantic relationship. Then I met David and we hit it off easily and immediately and I realized I'd been selling myself short. As for those emotional issues I'd been so worried about? Funny how they magically disappeared once I met the right guy! I'm a good wife and loving partner and I definitely have all the intimacy skills I need to be in a strong marriage.

— Felicia, 45

I know some of you don't believe me. You'd like to, really you would, but you don't. How can you possibly be okay just the way you are? It doesn't make sense. Most everyone you know is happily coupled up and you're not, so something *must* be wrong.

But despite your doubts, you're hanging in—giving me a chance to convince you. Occasionally you truly resonate with a theme, get caught up in the hype, and maybe even blurt out an audible "That's right!" or "You know it!" In those moments you feel totally supported and understood. You embrace the clear and obvious logic of "It just hasn't happened yet" and wonder why no one has ever pulled back the curtain on this issue before. It's time we let single women off the hook!

But then the backlash—that familiar defeatist thinking rears its head, scourging you with doubts and flat-out rejection of my premise. *What does she know anyway? It took Karin forever to meet her husband! She's probably an emotional wreck herself. Please, it's the blind leading the blind! All this book does is tick off items on a single woman's Wish List. We wish we were okay as is. We wish we weren't messed up. We wish we could believe single is the new black. But come on, who are we kidding? Sometimes people truly sabotage their love lives or can't even get into decent relationships in the first place because they're blocked by fears of intimacy or they have trust issues or some other sort of screwed up condition. You're a psychologist, Karin! You should know that!*

I hear you and I get it. I do. I know it's hard to fight the onslaught of negative messages we assimilated long ago from sources we perceived as trustworthy and reliable. And sure, I understand the power of dysfunction and neurosis. In fact, some might find it rather surprising that a psychologist would take a stance of "You're fine the way you are." After all, I've been trained to do the exact opposite—to diagnose maladaptive cognitions and problematic behavior.

But I won't do it here. I refuse to label women as pathological based solely on the criterion of their marital status. And I certainly won't construct formulaic treatment plans guaranteed to bring about everlasting love and happiness. Such an approach might work for depression or obsessive-compulsive disorder, but in the case of single women and their love lives, it's completely illogical.

PSYCH 101: WHY WE DO IT

We challenge the "It just hasn't happened yet" message because it's a new concept for us, and old habits—in this case, habitual ways of thinking—die hard. Adjusting our cognitive default settings requires an enormous amount of effort. And some of us just can't let go of the idea that we need to change something about ourselves before we'll be ready for Mr.

Right. As we discussed in chapter 1, it's a control thing. I understand.

That being said, I'm not trying to assert that single women should slack off and abandon any efforts toward self-improvement. Not in the least! If you're unhappy with an aspect of your life, by all means, address it. Irritated by some annoying tendency or trait? Fix it! Got issues? Work through them! Looking for insight into who you are? See a therapist! I'm all for self-exploration and edification. Attend a motivational seminar, take a meditation class, hire a life coach, or reconnect with the religious upbringing of your youth. Become whoever it is you're meant to become. But please don't expect some sort of karmic exchange, *à la I cleaned up my act and addressed* [insert pet pathology here] *so I've done my part. Now my man is sure to show up!*

It just hasn't happened yet

Still don't believe me? Can't get on board with the idea that you're fine just the way you are? Let me put it another way.

Self-help reasoning (or that of anyone else who's weighing in) assumes single women possess pesky imperfections and eccentricities which prevent us from snagging a man. So by this line of thinking, such personality shortcomings would appear much less frequently in the population of happily married women, right?

Doubtful. Ask any husband—he'll tell you. Wives show a full range of behaviors, quirks, and idiosyncrasies, just like the rest of us. After all, they may be wives, but they're still human.

Even better, many of our happily married friends exhibit extreme versions of the very traits that supposedly stymie our success. Often, in fact, these characteristics constitute key elements in their marital dynamics. Observe any couple. It doesn't take a degree in psychology to note the complementary nature of compatibility. Nutty women find husbands who like drama queens. Needy women secure men who enjoy being needed. If the match occurs at the expected time in a woman's life (typically in her mid-to-late twenties) everyone smiles, applauds, and buys a place setting off her gift registry. No one cares that the bride's a little loopy or that she lacks even a shred of self-reliance. No one mentions the neuroses cementing the marital union. No one frets about Little Miss Nutty or Little Miss Needy because they've become Little *Mrs.* Nutty and Little *Mrs.* Needy.

But a single woman with the exact same instability issues as Little Mrs. Nutty or the dependency issues of Little Mrs. Needy is suspect. With the best intentions, others tell her she better do some soul searching to figure out what's wrong—

what's keeping her single. Is this a fair analysis? Or more importantly, is it even remotely accurate? Hardly! Yet, every day single women yield to this nonsense, feeling cruddy and inferior.

Ditto

In preparing for this chapter, I interviewed women who'd been there—women who remained single longer than they'd expected, who'd endured periods of self-doubt along the way, acknowledging that, at times, they'd wondered what the problem was, why love seemed so hard to find. Each woman stated emphatically that she wished she'd known then what she knows now—that there was *nothing* wrong with her whatsoever—it just hadn't happened yet.

I asked them to provide some words of wisdom in the form of a quote that had inspired them during their single years. Here are some of my favorites:

"It's a funny thing about life: if you refuse to accept anything but the very best, you will very often get it."
                                        — W. Somerset Maugham

"Don't compromise yourself. You are all you've got."
                                        — Janis Joplin

"Living in the moment means letting go of the past and not waiting for the future. It means living your life consciously, aware that each moment you breathe is a gift."

— Oprah Winfrey

"I've learned from experience that the greater part of our happiness or misery depends on our dispositions and not on our circumstances."

— Martha Washington

"Only when we are no longer afraid do we begin to live."

— Dorothy Thompson

"We must be willing to get rid of the life we've planned, so as to have the life that is waiting for us."

— Joseph Campbell

Girl Talk

Dear Karin,

Let me take a moment to weigh in as "one who's been there". As a single woman living in New York during my 20s and 30s, I heard every explanation in the proverbial book (and those from your book, as a matter of fact) as to why I was unattached.

Did I get tired of all the unsolicited advice and lame prescriptions to treat my "problem"? Definitely! And of course people told me I was "too picky" but I was okay with that because I refused to consider spending my life with someone who didn't really fit the bill. So I waited for the right one, but he took his time showing up, and I didn't get married until I was 43.

Personally, I think that smart and accomplished women have it harder because many men seem to want to dominate. But that's all the more reason to wait for the right one, a guy who can really appreciate your intelligence and accomplishments. You want a partner, after all, not a daddy or a kid to care for.

But for me, because it took so long to find the right guy, I had to give up my desire to have children. That's a very real sacrifice. I did try to get pregnant on my own in my late 30s via a sperm bank, and when that didn't work and I was faced with considering more invasive procedures, I had to do some real soul-searching. Finally I decided that I would rather have a good partner than a child by myself (because it would probably become even harder to find someone if I were a parent). But that is in the mix there, too. And I think when we get to a certain age women may have to make that choice.

— *Erin, 48*

Dear Erin,

Hmmm. So I intended for this chapter to substantiate my point with testimonies of women who withstood the pressure to settle and ended up happily married, even if it took longer than they expected. But you bring up a very real concern and one I haven't touched on.

And maybe I haven't dealt with it because it's a sad, not-so-encouraging reality of the single woman's journey. By waiting for the right guy we may miss out on the chance to have it all. Like you said, some of us might have to make a choice at some point. Do we freeze our eggs, hoping Mr. Right will eventually show? Or find a sperm donor and try to get pregnant solo? Should we marry the okay guy we're dating because he'll make a good father?

It's hard to talk about because it stinks to think that a woman who did the right thing by waiting for the right husband, a woman who is emotionally stable and economically secure and who wants to be a mother, wouldn't get the chance to be one. Unfortunately, your experience clearly shows that sometimes that's what happens. It's tough and unfair and I'm sorry.

— Karin

The Awful Truth

Remember, these scenes are not *based* on real stories. They *are* real stories!

LOVE ENOUGH FOR BOTH?

CAST.
JANE: 32-year-old grad student, engaged to be married
VANESSA: 35-year-old grad student and Jane's classmate

INTERIOR — CONDOMINIUM IN THE CITY — DAY

Jane and Vanessa are in the midst of an intense discussion. Jane has been crying and is trying to compose herself.

> JANE
>
> It's not that I don't love my fiancé, Vanessa. I *do*. It's just that it doesn't feel quite right. But what does *right* feel like, anyway?

> VANESSA
>
> This may be hard to hear, Jane, but I can tell you I had similar

misgivings before I married my
first husband.

JANE

I didn't know you were married
before.

VANESSA

Oh, yeah. I had a starter
marriage a few years ago.

JANE

Really? What happened?

VANESSA

Well, he was perfect—at least on
paper. Derek had a great job, lots
of money, owned a couple homes—
the whole nine yards. And I had
just turned 30 and my parents
were pressuring me and everyone
was like, "What's the matter?
Why aren't you married yet?"
You know, the typical stuff single
women hear. Plus, I was really
anxious to have children and was
scared that time was running out.
So I guess in a way I gave in to
their expectations and my fear of
never becoming a mom.

JANE

What happened?

VANESSA

Well, we got engaged and I was a complete wreck the entire time—horrible jitters and cold feet. I was dreading the wedding, but went through with it anyway because, you know, I'd waited long enough for "Mr. Right" so "Mr. Pretty Close and Wealthy" would have to do. Plus he was crazy about me. I guess I figured he loved me enough for both of us.

JANE

But it didn't last, huh?

VANESSA

Nope. His love was enough for both of us until I met a struggling documentary filmmaker who made my heart do back flips. How's that old song go? "It's sad to belong to someone else when the right one comes along." Well it is. And it was.

Lesson learned: Let's skip the starter marriages and early divorces. How 'bout we spend our man-free time enjoying who we are and learning about who we're becoming? Take it from those who've been there—it's best to wait for the right one.

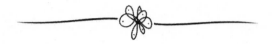

Guy Talk

It's that Biological Clock thing again, isn't it? Of course guys can never quite understand it. How could we? Our little swimmers stay strong into our 60s and 70s so fatherhood is something we can wait on.

Now as for this "choice thing" Erin's talking about—Karin addressed it a little in the "Too Picky" chapter and I didn't weigh in on it then, but I'm going to now.

Hear me loud and clear, ladies. Just wait for the right guy already! I mean, freeze your eggs if you want to or find yourself a sperm donor; I don't have a problem with any of that. But the one option I'd ask you <u>not</u> to consider is settling for some dude just because you think he'd be a good father. Because that's not really fair to the guy now is it?

This really hit me a while ago with a woman I was dating. She was smart, funny, successful, beautiful, had a great group of friends, and a very full life. She also happened to be a few years older than I and had just turned 39. She was incredibly energetic and upbeat about life in general, but every once in a while she'd get real down. And when I'd ask her what was wrong, she'd be like, "I don't have a baby and the chances of me ever having one are getting slimmer and slimmer and it's depressing." Of course I tried to listen and be sensitive, and I'd remind her that she'd made a lot of choices in her life that had brought her to this place. Um, apparently that was the WRONG thing to say because she'd go through the roof! She said I had no clue what motherhood meant to a woman and you know what? I think she was right.

We broke up a few months later and I don't think it was because of that, but I do have to say that, although we weren't very compatible, I felt like she might have kept on with me because I represented maybe her last chance to have a kid. And that didn't sit well with me at all.

233

So, like I said, don't do that to your boyfriend. Guys want to be loved for themselves, not for their sperm.

— Guy

Guy,

Let me get this out of the way first: If telling a 39-year-old woman that it's her fault she's single and childless is your idea of being sensitive, we really need to have a heart-to-heart! I know you, so I understand you were trying to be supportive, but, trust me, all you did was make her feel way worse.

And clearly you get it—that there's no way you can completely understand what being a mother means to a woman. Motherhood and fatherhood are vastly different constructs in our culture (and probably in most other cultures, too). You can't really imagine how much pressure we feel to procreate. We're hit with the "mommy mandate" early and often. While little boys play with trucks and beat each other up at recess, we feed our baby dolls, put them down for naps, and change their diapers. The vast majority of us never considered the possibility of *not* being mothers someday. And even if we love our careers and adore our friends and think we have utterly fantastic lives, most of us will have to grieve the loss of not having children if that is, in fact, the hand we're dealt.

I suppose we got off topic a bit, but Erin brought it up and I didn't want to ignore the subject. That's not fair to do when it's a reality some of us will face.

— Karin

Selfie

When I published the first edition of this book, I was 40 years old without a man in sight. I get it. I've been there, done that. I understand exactly what you put up with trying to navigate your way through the jungle that is the singles' scene. So even before I'd found my own happily ever after, I knew I had to speak to these issues and encourage my fellow single ladies. Now that I've met The One, I'm even more passionate about inspiring women to stay strong and hopeful. Keep believing that a great love can come your way! Don't succumb to the ridiculous messages you hear, and by all means, *never ever* settle!

Recently, my bestie, Caroline, who was one of the first to read my book, texted me, "I'm starting to go in and out of anxiety about finding someone. I'm 31! Time goes fast!"

"Read my book again and let's get together soon," I replied. "I'll talk you off the ledge."

We all need pep talks now and again—a shot in

the arm to remind us of what we know deep down but need to hear again. Even my BFF, who has read my book and listens to me rant about this stuff all the time, still struggles to hang onto the truth—she's fine the way she is and it just hasn't happened yet!

But I remember those feelings all too well. In fact, as you now know, at Caroline's age I had so much anxiety about finding someone I continued to date Dave, though my heart wasn't in it. I fell prey to the messages we've identified in this book, doubting myself in myriad ways. I feared the intense romantic connection I searched for was mere fantasy—the stuff of chick flicks and fairytales. Essentially, I gave up. I figured, *Some women find the love of their life. Others marry a really good guy and make the best of it.*

How I needed a word of hope and encouragement from those who'd been there!

Shout Out!

So to my smart, sexy, savvy singletons I say this: Millions of women can attest to the fact that it'll happen eventually. Don't create a mess by rushing into something because you've given up hope. Refuse to accept anything but the best and watch it come your way. So many women *wish* they were in your shoes because they settled and now they're stuck. But not you! Stay strong. Keep the faith... because single is the new black!

chapter 14

Get on with Your Fabulous Life!

you're no "Lady in Waiting"

My friends are always giving me the "Your time will come" line. As if I'm just stuck in some dead-end waiting room, holding a ticket, hoping that any moment my number will be called and then my life can suddenly begin and I'll be happy! It makes me want to rip out my hair every time... and then, how am I gonna get a guy without any hair?

— Corrine, 27

So sneaky, so subtle, so surreptitious. We don't even know we're doing it, but we are. Even if we do become aware of it, we still probably think it's okay. Unless someone challenges us on it, we see no need to change. But it keeps us miserable, detached, and, arguably, half alive.

When I get a boyfriend... When I get engaged... When it's my wedding... When I get pregnant... When I have a family... When! When! When! Living for *when*—what a waste of a life!

238

And yet so many single women adopt this "Lady in Waiting" stance. We put our lives on hold until the *whens* occur. Nothing we do matters all that much until we can check these objectives off the list. Until then, we float in limbo. Sure we look like we're living, but we're not. We're *waiting*.

"Ladies in Waiting" fall along various points on a wide continuum. In some cases, a woman postpones normal, age-appropriate life decisions and completely avoids participating in certain events. She eats off paper plates in lieu of purchasing dinnerware since she'll eventually register for everything once she's engaged and what if her future husband wants to weigh in on the flatware and stemware selections? Others put off vacation plans. Who wants to go to Paris with girlfriends? Everyone knows it's a city for lovers. This "Lady in Waiting" maintains she'd rather save the trip for her honeymoon.

A more flagrant, yet unfortunately not uncommon, variation of the "Lady in Waiting" mindset causes a woman to essentially live the life she *expects* to have one day, while thoroughly minimizing and dismissing the life she *actually lives*. She's the gal with more baby toys in her apartment than furniture. In preparation for motherhood, she's been stocking up on items from *Pottery Barn Kids* and *Janie and Jack* for years. At 30, she still furnishes her living room with cinder block book shelves but has shelled out $15,000 to outfit a second bedroom into the most charming nursery! Granted, she has neither husband nor baby in sight, but that's just a slight technicality.

But by far the most debilitating and insidious infestation of the "Lady in Waiting" mentality plagues most of us most of the time in an ongoing mental commentary. Overtly, we live our lives—make adult purchases and take grown-up vacations—but a continuous clandestine commentary exposes our true attitudes:

- On our way to buy dinnerware: *This would be so much more fun if I were picking out china patterns with my fiancé and not stuck doing this all alone.*

- With our friends at a café on the Champs-Élysées: *Paris! The City of Lights! How romantic! Everything would be perfect if this were a getaway with my gorgeous husband. Too bad I'm just here with the girls.*

- Strolling through the mall: *I know it would be stupid to buy this Vera Bradley diaper bag now, but I really wish I were in the market for one.*

When will I get my chance to be a mom?
[sigh]

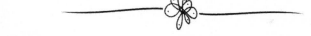

PSYCH 101: WHY WE DO IT

It's simple, really. With the placing of a pink crocheted bonnet on our newborn heads, the programming and conditioning commenced. As little girls, every fairy tale we heard began with *Once upon a time* and ended with *happily ever after*—and not once did *happily ever after* occur without a prince. In adolescence, *Seventeen* magazine convinced us our "Dream Prom" necessitated a "Dream Date"—anything less would leave us less than happy; going stag or with girlfriends was clearly second best. And college merely upped the ante. Firmly indoctrinated in our women's studies, we gave lip service to feminist existentialism and consciousness raising, but that didn't assuage our angst that Homecoming loomed and we had yet to secure a date.

Throughout our formative years, in countless ways, our culture bombarded us with the message, "Your happiness won't be complete until you meet your man." And before we had the wherewithal to question or resist, we'd internalized this rigid philosophy, becoming bona fide "Ladies in Waiting".

It just hasn't happened yet

Okay, fine. We may have unwittingly inherited this philosophy, but we're older and wiser now. We know better. It's high time we protested this pitiful perspective. Assuming a "Lady in Waiting" stance is no way to live!

Every adage applies: "You only go around once in life." "This isn't a dress rehearsal." "All we have is the present moment." Clichés or not, they're true! My 8th grade English teacher used to say, "Time is life and life is time. If you waste time, you're committing suicide." She had a point—one that many single women should take to heart. If we embrace a "Lady in Waiting" mentality, we commit a slow form of suicide.

Perhaps that seems a tad drastic, but think about your stance on life and time. Do we savor every phase, enjoying all the wonderful things happening *right now*? Or do we wish our lives away, judging our own existence as inferior until a man materializes to legitimize us? Do we create full and exciting lives, utilizing the breadth of our gifts, talents, and abilities? Or do we passively squander precious hours, days, and months waiting for the *whens*? Do we relish our amazing friendships and family connections, or do we minimize these relationships, refusing to be happy with just about anything in our lives until we snag a husband?

Waiting, waiting, waiting, for The One. But what if he never shows up? What does that make—a worthless life? If you consent to the "Lady in Waiting" philosophy, that's essentially what you're asserting. Are you prepared to say that about yourself and your single girlfriends? Why would you want to?

It's a choice. Simple as that. A choice. You can choose to plod through every day, crossing it off on your calendar, thankful only to make it one step closer to the day you find your man. Or you can approach life as an adventure you create for yourself—on your terms and according to your ideology and standards. It's up to you.

If you're ready to chuck the "Lady in Waiting" mentality, here are a few tenets to try on for size. They should ring a bell—each one reflects a theme from this book:

- So I'm single. So what? It's not my fault or anything. Plus, single is the new black!

- My mother lived her life and I'm living mine. Of course she harbors some hopes and dreams for me, but I'm not about to cave to pressure just to guarantee her a couple grandkids.

- Yeah, maybe I am picky and I intend to stay that way!

- Listen, I'm as "out there" as I'm ever gonna get, so deal with it!

- Tone it down? What a ridiculous concept! It would *never* occur to me to be anything less than my fabulous self.

- When it comes to love, trying or not trying is hardly the issue—it just hasn't happened yet.

- Everyone travels a unique journey in life. I refuse to compare myself to my friends. Where they are right now is great for them; where I am right now is great for me. I'm not worried about keeping up with Joan or Lily or Kaitlyn.

- If I want to do some online dating, I will. But I won't feel compelled or obligated.

- I expect a future full of boyfriends who will blow my ex-boyfriends out of the water. No time for regressing into the ex-fray.

- I have many fascinating and intriguing things to think about each day. I may reflect on relationships, but I won't waste good neural energy *obsessing* about men.

- I'm alone because I'm strong enough to wait for the right one and I refuse to settle!

- I'll handle my quest for love *my* way on *my* terms. When I feel like making an effort, I will. When I don't, I won't.

- When frustrated, I'll look to the women who've been there—who have heard all the nonsense I hear, but who stuck to their guns and waited for the right guy.

- I value my life and myself for who I am—not who I'm with. I'm living to the fullest now!

And of course, if a wonderful man shows up and you decide to let him come along for the ride, fantastic. Lucky him! And then, just like that, it will have happened.

Ditto

In their book, *Last One Down The Aisle Wins*, authors Shannon Fox and Celeste Liversidge urge readers to chuck the "bridal wars", and *plan* on marrying *later*.

"Here's the key: Don't marry young. If you're serious about improving your chances of choosing a great husband and having a fabulous marriage, there's a lot you need to be doing *now*, before you walk down the rose-petaled aisle.

The choices we make before we're married, even long before we lay our eyes on our spouse, have the biggest impact on the success or failure of our future marriage... happy marriages are born out of fulfilled single lives."[28]

Recent research studies support their view. Economist Dana Rotz finds that, "for every year a woman waits to marry, she lowers her risk of divorce." Specifically, women who marry for the first time between the ages of 35 and 39 are 46% less likely to divorce than those women who marry between the ages of 23 and 26. Rotz's study did not contain enough data to conclude if this trend continues for marriages after age 40, but she believes it's likely.[29]

Girl Talk

Dear Karin,

Yeah, yeah, yeah. I know you're right, and I get that it's lame to be a "Lady in Waiting" and all, but you make it sound so easy and it's NOT! I mean, come on! It <u>is</u> more fun to pick out plates if someone other than you is going to eat off them and it <u>is</u> way better to be in the most romantic city in the world with a guy than with the girls and it <u>is</u> tempting to buy diaper bags even when you're single—especially if they're Vera Bradley!

Plus, this year has been the worst because I've been in—count 'em—four weddings and it's tough not dreaming about my own wedding while helping my girls with theirs. Is that so wrong? So what if I've already bought my wedding planner, picked out my color palette, selected my bridal party and chosen the song my husband and I will dance to during the reception. I'm just getting caught up in the hype. And no, I don't have a boyfriend right now, but I want to be prepared for when that day comes!

— Missy, 27

Dear Missy,

You've got the living in the "whens" thing down pat, don't you? With your "have wedding, insert groom" mentality, you'll be more than ready when that day comes—which, admittedly, will be quite efficient because you'll already have finished a lot of the wedding prep so you'll be able to really enjoy your engagement and not be so stressed out.

But at the same time, have you thought about how your groom will feel knowing you picked out a song representing your undying love for each other when you didn't even know who the heck he was? Seems a bit odd to me, but, hey, I'm not trying to spoil your fun or anything.

And if it is, in fact, fun for you, then tell me to shut up and I'll back off, but I can't help but wonder why you're giving all this time in your twenties—time that should be all about *you*, enjoying *you*, discovering *you*—to some man you've never met and to a love you have yet to experience.

I wonder if it's a case of no one around you validating your life right now, so you devalue it, too. Maybe with all your girls getting married, there's no room to appreciate anything other than the "accomplishment" of matrimony. All other undertakings—work achievements, travels, educational pursuits—are simply consolation prizes. I can relate.

In my late twenties, I began pursuing a doctorate in psychology. Now I'm definitely a bit sensitive, but I remember feeling that when people learned what I was doing they were interested and impressed—which was great, of course—but I also sensed that at least of some of them questioned whether I'd be working on a graduate degree if my personal life were in a different place. Almost a "*well, it's nice she's filling up her time with school since she doesn't have a husband and children...*"

Again, my thin skin may have bruised a bit too easily, but my point is I know how it feels when friends unintentionally devalue your life. And you might be constructing your TBA-wedding with your TBA-groom in efforts to stay in the loop with your friends—to be where they are and a part of their scene—because that's what matters to them. But in the end, you're just disparaging your life, your circumstances, and ultimately, yourself.

— Karin

The Awful Truth

Remember, these scenes are not *based* on real stories. They *are* real stories!

YOU CAN'T RUSH A GOOD THING

CAST.
TAMMY: 21-year-old, college junior
KRISTIN: Tammy's best friend and roommate

INTERIOR — COLLEGE DORM ROOM — DAY

Kristin is headed to class and has accidentally grabbed some of Tammy's notebooks. She's flipping through them when Tammy walks in.

                    KRISTIN
You've got some explaining to do, girlfriend.

                    TAMMY
What are you talking about?

                    KRISTIN
I'm not sure, but let's see if we can make sense of it. You and Paul started dating, what? Two weeks ago? And now you've devoted an entire page of your Sociology notebook to sketching out your wedding party and writing variations of your new name—"Tammy Bates Hutchinson"

and "Mr. and Mrs. Paul Hutchinson"? Seriously?

TAMMY

So what?

KRISTIN

So what? That's totally lame! That's what!

TAMMY

I know, I know. I'm supposed to be all Ms. Independent and stuff, but I can't help it. I get excited about being married someday. And honestly, I just don't feel complete without a guy. I'm not the only one, you know. Women are made that way, Kristin!

KRISTIN

Hey, there's nothing wrong with wanting to get married someday, but may I remind you that you're only 21 years old and you've been dating Paul for all of two weeks? And may I also remind you that a few years ago there was this thing called Women's Liberation and women of our generation are supposed to be the beneficiaries of the changes this movement brought about.

                    TAMMY
Huh? You lost me.

                    KRISTIN
No kidding! Maybe if you paid a little more attention in Sociology, you might know what I'm talking about.

Kristin pauses and shakes her head.

                    KRISTIN
But, hey, thanks for the maid-of-honor nod. Should I get fitted for my gown right away or wait another two weeks till you're officially engaged?

Lesson Learned: Some "Ladies in Waiting" won't respond to interventions. Refusing to acknowledge their worth *sans* husbands, they hold out on life while holding out for Mr. Right. Our fabulousness is a choice, you know. We decide it, create it, and live it. Or we don't. But *we* determine our value and *we* ascribe meaning to who we are and what we're about.

Guy Talk

This is another one that's hard for me to get. And it's probably because of all the stuff Karin keeps harping on—how men and women are socialized differently and that a man's worth is determined by his career and income, but women remain judged by the man they're with. And even as I write that I think, "Really? Still? That's so lame!" But I've read this whole book, too, and I guess Karin convinced me along the way. (Yes! We got through to him! — Karin)

That being said, I certainly hope things begin to change. Maybe this generation of men can help improve things for the future. I mean, I think about being a father someday and how I'll instill everything I can into my daughter. And of course she'll be talented, intelligent, ambitious, and charismatic and I'll adore her and tell her how wonderful she is. So I'd hate to think that somehow she wouldn't really believe herself to be all these things unless she was dating some dude. I mean, what about the father who loves and adores her? My opinion doesn't matter? The only thing that makes her feel worthwhile is if she's arm-and-arm with some guy with a slick suit, gelled-up hair, and

impressive résumé? I am *not* okay with that! She could end up rushing to marry some bonehead just to keep up with the Joans and earn society's blessing but then be miserable for the rest of her life! Have you thought about *that?* This has got to stop!

— Guy

Well yes, Guy, we have thought about that. It's basically what I've been talking about for the last couple hundred pages. But that was really sweet. You're not even a father yet and you're already championing your daughter's value and worth. I love it!

— Karin

Selfie

Writers are told to write what they know and that's what I've done. Every ounce of counsel I've given you in this book comes from the myriad pitfalls I stumbled into during my 27 years of dating. I, too, occasionally slipped into the "Lady in Waiting" trap, devaluing my single life and living for "when". Ultimately, that's how I almost married the wrong man.

As the wedding approached, I waged an

agonizing internal battle. Thoughts of, *I can't go through with this! It doesn't feel right!* combatted an opposing belief, *If you don't marry Dave, you might be single forever. You're already 34. This could be your last chance to be a mom.* I, myself, often wondered which side would win.

A week before my first shower, the inner tumult came to a head. I literally and figuratively looked myself in the mirror and said, *Here's the deal, Karin. If you cancel the wedding you may never have another chance to marry and have a family. That's a real possibility and you've got to fully accept it and deal with it. But deep down you know you'd rather stay single and remain true to yourself than marry a man you're not in love with and live a lie.*

That was it. Once I acknowledged that living a phony life wasn't an option for me, I could pull the trigger and cancel the wedding. I *finally* listened to what my gut had been telling me all along.

Though initially wracked with guilt and remorse for hurting Dave, eventually I recognized I actually did him an enormous favor. By breaking things off, I freed him up to find a woman who would love him the way he deserved to be loved—as opposed to someone like me, who was marrying him because I was 34 and it was time, and I guess he'd do.

Calling off my wedding proved a watershed moment for me. It ultimately changed my mindset forever. Not to say I had everything figured out, but running away from the altar showed me what I was made of in ways no other experience could. I'll always wish I could have exited the relationship sooner, releasing Dave before things moved so far along. But for whatever reason, it took almost marrying the wrong man to finally realize that I hadn't met The One for me and that, no matter what, I would *never, ever* settle. It just hadn't happened yet.

Shout Out!

So to my smart, sexy, savvy singletons I say this: You've got a fabulous life going on—if only you'll grab onto it! No living for "when"! No "Ladies in Waiting"! No disparaging your single status. You're tough enough to go it alone and strong enough not to settle! Not everyone can handle that, you know? But you can and you do and you know it just hasn't happened yet. Which is perfectly fine... because single is the new black!

Epilogue

In writing this book I adamantly refused to prescribe a blueprint for finding a man.

Too many authors profess to have all the answers. The last thing we needed in the Dating/Relationship genre was another self-help text berating single women for screwing up their love lives. Besides, I knew these books couldn't make good on their claims because I'd read most of them, tried their tactics, yet there I was, 40 and still single.

So I wrote my own book—which *didn't* pretend to have all the answers—and met my husband three months after I published it. Go figure.

Please understand, I'm not trying to tell you what to do. But then again, most of you hope to meet The One someday and, since happily-ever-after eventually came my way, I figured you might want to know how it happened for me.

"You're such a sweet girl, and bright and pretty! I don't understand why you're not married!"

If I had a dollar for every time I heard comments like this over the years! I know people meant it as a compliment but to me it felt more like an insult—like, "Get your act together, girl. You're obviously doing something wrong!"

Besides, how do you respond to that? I didn't have any answers—especially since I often wondered the same thing! I worried, too, fearing that maybe people were right—there was something wrong with me, something keeping me single.

Twenty-seven years of dating trying to figure out why love eluded me...

But now I *finally* have the answer. Are you ready? Want to know why I was single for so long?

Wait for it...

It just hadn't happened yet.

Because the love of my life was married to someone else. Simple as that.

There wasn't anything wrong with me—at least nothing directly responsible for my single status. Like every other human being on the planet, I possess a full range of strengths and weaknesses and, like most people, I try to work on my negative qualities. But none of these traits kept me single. It just hadn't happened yet. I didn't need to change some man-repelling quality or conduct a comprehensive personality overhaul because—I'll say it again—it just hadn't happened yet.

And by the way, my husband is super glad I didn't change who I was in order to snag a guy. He loves me *exactly* the way I am. Seriously, he absolutely adores me and I'm here to tell you, it feels incredible to be cherished for who I am. Take that, all you cruddy self-help books that tried to get me to change!

Man, I wish I'd known this at 35 when I was caught up in relentless self-analysis trying to figure out what I was doing wrong. What a big, fat waste of time and energy! There was no way for me to speed things up or remedy my love life because the man I was meant to be with simply wasn't available. I had to wait for my husband to exit a marriage that wasn't working, join a dating service, and walk into a wine bar on Michigan Avenue. Once he did all that—it happened!

Actually, I take it back. I said I was like every other human being on the planet and that's mostly true, but in one significant way I am different. Some people settle. I refused to. And I'm *so* glad I didn't.

Five Steps to Meeting The One

For real, I can sum it up in 5 steps:

1) Be thankful and excited about all the great things going on in your life—because your marital status does *not* define you.

2) Maintain high standards for important qualities and lose unreasonable expectations, *i.e.* He doesn't have to be 6 feet tall, with 6 pack abs, and make 6 figures, but he *does* have to be kind,

loving, and full of integrity.

3) Stay positive, hopeful, and happy—because that's your job anyway. Marriage doesn't make you happy; *you* make you happy.

4) Know it's *way* better to be single than in a mediocre marriage.

5) Never EVER settle!

Afterword

Thanks for picking up the book and giving it a read. I hope you've been encouraged, emboldened, and empowered! Ideally, the next time someone says something insensitive (or flat-out stupid) about you being single, you'll think back to the themes we've discussed here and laugh it off with a, "Whatever! It just hasn't happened yet and besides, single is the new black!"

If you want to join the conversation, check out my website, DrKarin.me, where you'll find a page devoted to *Single is the New Black*. Download the book club questions or check out my blog posts and articles which reinforce the themes of this book.

If there's a dilemma you're facing, click on the "Ask Dr. Karin" link and I'll personally answer your dating/relationship questions.

Please follow me on Facebook, Twitter, and Instagram so we can stay connected!

DR. KARIN

Acknowledgments

I am deeply and forever indebted to my parents, Dr. Simon and Nancy Anderson, who, by their example, taught me to live each day to its fullest, dream big dreams, and find, no matter what life throws at me, a way to "get happy". Thanks to my brothers—Warren, for frequent and skillful editing, and Elliott, who inspired me to "make it happen" by writing his own book.

Much gratitude to my team—my editor at Clifton Hills Press, Colleen McSwiggin, for believing in my message and bringing a keen mind and sharp focus to this project, also my stellar publicist, Daphne Ortiz, for enthusiasm, drive, and help with the new title, and my assistant, Sydney Shrum, for clever social media strategies and keeping me in touch with my inner twenty-something.

Thanks to the many single women who graciously shared their stories with me. Your candor gave this book its voice.

Finally, a big smooch to my husband Dan, for proving me right! You were absolutely worth the wait and I'm so thankful I never *ever* settled! *It's like breathing, so easy. Loving you couldn't come more naturally.*

Works Cited

[1] Daley, N. (2014, September 11). "Single? So are the majority of US adults." *The Rundown*. Retrieved from http://www.pbs.org/newshour/rundown/single-youre-not-alone/

[2] De Paulo, B. (2006). *Singled out: How singles are stereotyped, stigmatized, and ignored and still live happily ever after*. New York: St. Martin's Press.

[3] De Paulo, B. (2006). *Singled out: How singles are stereotyped, stigmatized, and ignored and still live happily ever after*. New York: St. Martin's Press.

[4] Scholssberg, S. (2004). *The curse of the singles table: A true story of 1001 nights without sex*. New York: Warner Books.

[5] Trimberger, E.K. (2005). *The new single woman*. Boston: Beacon Press.

[6] Wedge, M. (2012). *Pills are not for preschoolers*. New York: Norton.

[7] Talbot, L. (2007, Aug. 21). "Stop Singlism!" *Forbes.com*. Retrieved from http://www.forbes.com/2007/08/21/talbot-singles-discrimination-forbeslife-singles07_cx_lt_0821talbot.html

[8] Trimberger, E.K. (2005). *The new single woman*. Boston: Beacon Press.

[9] Cochrane, K. (2006). "Marriage and terrorism—a dangerous mix". *Guardian.co.uk*. Retrieved from http://www.guardian.co.uk/world/2006/jun/01/gender.lifeandhealth

[10] Harris, L. (2006). "*Newsweek*: OK, singles, now you can worry about terrorism". *Salon*. Retrieved from http://www.salon.com/life/broadsheet/2006/05/24/newsweek_marriage/index.html

[11] Frank-Ruta, G. (2002, June 18). "Creating a lie". *The American Prospect* Retrieved from https://prospect.org/article/creating-lie

[12] Whelan, C. (2006). *Why smart men marry smart women.* New York: Simon & Schuster.

[13] Irvine, A. (2009, Nov. 11). "Thanks but I don't need you to hook me up". *CNN.com*. Retrieved from http://www.cnn.com/2009/LIVING/personal/11/11/rrants.exhibit.a/index.html

[14] De Paulo, B. (2006). *Singled out: How singles are stereotyped, stigmatized, and ignored and still live happily ever after.* New York: St. Martin's Press.

[15] De Paulo, B. (2006). *Singled out: How singles are stereotyped, stigmatized, and ignored and still live happily ever after.* New York: St. Martin's Press.

[16] Greenwald, M. (n.d.) "Being credentialed". *UnmarriedAmerica.org*. Retrieved from http://www.unmarriedamerica.org/beingcred.html

[17] Rupersburg, N. (2015, April 20). "Why I hate online dating: I get that it's practical. It's just not for me". *Cosmopolitan.com* Retrieved from http://www.cosmopolitan.com/sex-love/news/a39293/why-i-hate-online-dating/

[18] Berman, L. (2008, July 3). "Can't quit your ex? How to say goodbye for good: You're better off alone! Don't get stuck in a 'make up/break up'." *MSNBC.com* Retrieved from http://today.msnbc.msn.com/id/25335116/ns/today-today_relationships/print/1/displaymode/1098/

[19] Lue, N. (2005). "Stop obsessing over how men communicate". *Baggage Reclaim*. Retrieved from http://www.baggagereclaim.co.uk/stop-obsessing-over-how-men-communicate/

[20] Martin, L. (2014, September 24). "21 things every woman needs to stop overanalyzing before they ruin her life". *Elite Daily*. Retrieved from http://elitedaily.com/women/25-things-women-analyze-need-stop/770918/

[21] Goodwin, P., McGill, B., & Anjani, C. (2009, June). "Who marries and when? Age at first marriage in the United States: 2002". *NCHA Data Brief, 19*. Retrieved from http://www.cdc.gov/nchs/data/databriefs/db19.pdf

[22] Lieberman, M. (2013). *Social: Why our brains are wired to connect.* New York: Crown.

[23] Ellis, A. (2001). *Overcoming destructive beliefs, feelings, and behaviors.* Amhurst, New York: Prometheus Books.

[24] Arylo, C. (2009). *Choosing me before we: Every woman's guide to life and love.* Novato, California: New World Library.

[25] Spielmann, S., MacDonald, G., Maxwell, J., Joel, S., Peragine, D., Muise, A., & Impett, E. (2013). "Settling for less out of fear of being single". *Journal of Personality and Social Psychology, 105,* 1049-1073.

[26] Spielmans, G., Berman, M, & Usitalo, A. (2011). "Psychotherapy versus second-generation antidepressants in the treatment of depression: A meta-analysis". *Journal of Nervous and Mental Diseases, 199,* 142-149.

[27] Eckel, S. (2014). *It's not you: 27 (wrong) reasons you're single.* New York: Penguin.

[28] Fox, S., & Liversidge, C. (2010). *Last one down the aisle wins: 10 keys to a fabulous single life now and an even better marriage later.* New York: Thomas Dunne Books.

[29] Rotz, D. (2011). "Why have divorce rates fallen? The role of women's age in marriage". Unpublished manuscript, Mathematica Policy Research, Inc., Harvard University, Cambridge, MA.

About the Author

Born in Cincinnati, Ohio, Karin Anderson Abrell holds a master's degree in clinical psychology and a doctorate in developmental psychology. She spent the early portion of her career as a psychotherapist for children in Chicago's child welfare system and then stepped into academia for ten years. As a professor, she delivered a number of well-received presentations at national and international psychology conferences, covering issues such as identity development and family dynamics.

Dr. Karin first became interested in writing about dating and relationships when examining the complex emotions involved in her own engagement to be married. As she questioned her motivations for marriage, she pondered women's roles and options in the post-feminism era. How much had really changed? After months of internal conflict, she called off her wedding two months before it was to occur.

Back "out there" in the dating scene, she became keenly aware of the messages directed toward single women—messages that appeared disparaging and illogical, yet hailed from reliable sources such as the local bookstore's self-help section. Drawing on the data of other academic researchers and first-hand accounts of the many women she interviewed personally, Dr.

Karin wrote *Single Is the New Black* in an effort to provide a logical counter-message of encouragement.

Practicing what she preaches, Karin waited for the right guy and didn't meet him until age 40. Two years later they were married and it finally "happened" for her.

A compelling presenter, Dr. Karin speaks to groups on single adulthood, identity issues, and family systems theory. For more information, visit DrKarin.me.